Better Business Development Now

Better Business Development Now: A Bare Bones Guide to Get More Clients!

Cameron M. Clark

Copyright © 2017 by Cameron M. Clark. All rights reserved.

Published by Paul St. George Press, Henderson, Nevada.

For information on how to share or reproduce parts of this book for informational purposes, please contact the author at www.cameronmclark.com/contact.

Legal Disclaimer: While the author and publisher have applied their best efforts while preparing this book, they make no representations or warranties with respect to the accuracy or completeness of the contents of this book and particularly disclaim any implied warranties of merchantability or fitness for a particular purpose. The advice and strategies that follow may not be suitable for your particular situation. You should consult with a professional when and where appropriate. The publisher and author disclaim responsibility for any adverse effects resulting directly or indirectly from the information that is contained in this book.

www.cameronmclark.com

ISBN-13: 978-1545331996
ISBN-10: 1545331995

For Cara & the Kiddos.

TABLE OF CONTENTS

INTRODUCTION	1
PREFACE	7
YOU!	13
YOUR STORY	17
MY STORY	19
DEFINITIONS	23
MY BARE BONES PHILOSOPHY	27
CUTTING CLOSE TO THE BONE - REJECTION	29
BETTER COMMUNICATION BASICS	33
BETTER COLD CALLING	45
8 BARE BONES TRAITS FOR BUSINESS DEVELOPMENT	57
GETTING COMMITMENTS	75
THE BARE BONES DON'TS TO ATTRACT NEW BUSINESS	101
THE BARE BONES DO'S TO ATTRACT NEW BUSINESS	109
REVIEW	127
I BELIEVE IN YOU	129
INVITATION	131
RECOMMENDED READING	133
ABOUT THE AUTHOR	137

INTRODUCTION

I have heard the following over and over again in my conversations with various professionals over the years:

"I hired an SEO expert to help me market my law firm, but it seems like most of my target clients lose interest in me after the initial consultation. Do I need to find a new SEO expert? Am I just wasting my money?"

"My payroll services company has done well for many years, but it was time for a rebrand. In the past, it has seemed to be a hit-or-miss proposition with prospective clients when I've tweaked the brand of the company. Some prospects signed up while others just fizzled out. How do I know if I am going in the right direction online?"

"I've never had a hard time getting people through the door or to pick up the phone to call me, but lately, it just seems like a lot of those relationships have fizzled. Maybe it's the changing times or the changing market. How do I get to where I can improve my business development strategies to create lasting

relationships? Is it a problem with the new customer relationship management software I installed?"

Sound familiar?

The focus on each of the above questions was always on creating more digital solutions, but they're each missing the point. They're based on the wrong premise. The solutions to your problems aren't clean-cut, calculated and technical; they're messy, varied and most of all, human.

Technologically speaking, we've come a long way in a short amount of time.

Society's technological achievements have seemed to reach a perceived pinnacle as the years stretch into the 21st Century. It's not over. There's more to come. There will always be more to come.

Every time we're led to believe we've reached the zenith of mechanized or electronic achievement, someone or something comes out of nowhere to surpass our original understanding of what was possible and blows it all up. Usually, something faster or more convenient is waiting just around the corner to make itself known. The intention of these application developers was to make things easier. Have these amazing advances made those things easier? More importantly, have they made life simpler?

I don't think the answer is so clear.

If it were, you would likely be making a profitable deal with every prospect you come in contact with because of the advantages your new software afforded to track relationships and relationship development.

Is that happening for you now?

Having worked for and with hundreds of professional services firms in legal support, collections, credit card processing and property management, along with running my own professional services company for a time, I have watched most leaders of every company focus solely on the concept of business growth. Winning new clients brings an unbelievable rush of excitement and adrenaline that is unparalleled in business, not to mention the new capital that comes your way of cash flow. It's the thrill of the hunt that excites so many business leaders.

Yet how does one win new business in this 21st Century economy? With the bevy of new information out there, you would think every professional service provider and every employee working for him or her would be an expert on the topic of winning business. And yet they aren't experts.

Why is that?

Many advances have been made in technology from mobile application development to social media networking to customer relationship management (CRM) software to statistical collection of website and application analytics. The way today's professional services provider measures and tracks the results of certain efforts or campaigns has become easier and yet more complicated all at the same time. Not all of these methods and advances are negative. In fact, there can be so many positive things that can result from these amazing technological advances when you are marketing and selling professional services.

Issues emerge when the tools or *means* to get new business becomes mixed up and is now seen as the *end* for getting new business. It can feel overwhelming.

When a focus on statistics related to a marketing campaign or how many clicks or 'likes' a social media post received becomes more important than actually receiving real life commitments from your clients to keep doing business with you, you've begun to fail. Tracking the clicks and stats can come in handy as long as they don't replace real life commitments between you and the client that translate into actual dollars for your firm.

That should be the real end for your business development process: attracting new clients who will repeatedly purchase your professional services and then refer their friends to your firm. Social media is just one of the many means to achieve that end.

After working in professional services sales, marketing, management and media for nearly 20 years, I have found that all of these advances in technology are hollow victories if they are missing one key component: the ability to connect with a client throughout the sales process and ultimately win the profitable deal that ensures he or she will hire and stay with your firm.

That is why I wrote this book.

The problem isn't really with having a social media presence, an Internet presence or even just getting the word out about your services. The problem arises when it comes to getting commitments from clients. It also arises when you choose not to keep your commitments. That is the essence of this book and the problem I want to help you solve.

I want to show you what I have learned, observed and practiced all of this time in my business development career. This book was written for attorneys, accountants, commercial insurance brokers, payroll specialists, commercial real estate agents and any other professionals who run a tight ship of only a few employees, but are looking for ways to augment their firm's efforts. You may run a small office or a large one. It doesn't really matter. The principles I share with you in this brief book can help you in getting the commitments you seek to grow your business. As I've told many of my clients in the past, my focus will be on progress, not perfection.

Beware of the desire for perfection. With a title like 'Better Business Development Now,' your goal should always be continual improvement, not ultimate perfection. Mark Twain said, 'Continual improvement is always better than delayed perfection.' No book, workshop, training system or otherwise will make your law firm or insurance agency perfect, but all of these resources can help make your company more profitable and a more efficient enterprise. Keep striving for that.

I know from personal experience that not having the sexiest website or slickest brochure can still lead to winning the deal. It's when you spend weeks or months obsessing over the size of the font in your brochures and color of the firm's logo on the company homepage that you are wasting time. You are avoiding the real work. Believe me, I've been there. Again, this is a matter of confusing the means with the end.

Professional people hire professional specialists to do professional work for them that they either don't have the time, the knowledge and/or the qualifications to perform themselves. Thus, they expect professional results. In this book, I focus on helping you develop the professional skills related to marketing and selling your services. More importantly, I help you work to get the commitments from the clients that you need to keep doing business with them after the thrill of the first 'yes' is a distant memory.

Not everyone will like this book. As I've already mentioned, this book should not be seen or treated as complete. What book that promises a 'bare bones' approach to business development could be considered complete? Nor will it ever be called a guide for dummies, because you dear reader, are not a dummy.

I wrote this book with your tough schedule in mind. It's brief and it's to the point. By my estimate, you should be able to read it in only a couple of sittings and it should take you a total of around 2 to 3 hours. That's about the same amount of time as it takes to watch a movie. Only the time here will be much better spent.

In the following pages, you will learn how to relate better to your prospective clients. You will also learn a basic process on how to get commitments from them that lead to more business for your professional firm. Along with that, I will share some practical ideas of what I have found worked for me when I ran my own professional services firm.

So, with that end in mind, let's get going!

PREFACE

I want to congratulate you and also thank you for being a professional.

Honestly, despite the higher income that most professional service providers are able to achieve in their practices, many still get disparaged and sometimes insulted blatantly when they tell an acquaintance about their occupation. We've all heard the lawyer jokes and the stereotypes about CPAs. There will be no shaming from me here. If any shame lingers, I invite you to purge the feeling now. You are a professional and in many cases, you are someone with an advanced education, trained to deliver professional services and results to clients who will gladly pay you a lot of money to solve their problems. The challenge is figuring out how to sell those services in a way that reflects your profession and more importantly, the dignified professional image you are seeking to convey.

I wrote the book I would have liked to read when I first got into professional services selling. For me, the concept for 'Better Business Development Now: A Bare Bones Guide to Get More Clients' came into existence because I couldn't find anything quite like it when I was a young, up-and-coming business development manager working for a litigation services support business in Las Vegas over a decade ago. It was frustrating to find so many books that covered basic sales techniques, but many of these books were written from the perspective of business-to-consumer selling rather than business-to-business sales.

Those books that did cover business-to-business selling were written by current or former professors, who'd left their ivory towers temporarily to converse with mere mortals and share their acquired theoretical wisdom in the hopes that there would be some practical way for these theories to be applied. In the process, some of them made loads of money consulting for Fortune 500 companies by applying their theoretical concepts. Needless to say, these books were dry, long and mostly esoteric in their approach to something as simple as selling. Some value was gained in my reading these, so it wasn't time wasted. However, my intent in writing this book for you is to save you some of the time, effort and agony of reading those books.

Here are some ideas to keep in mind as you read the following pages.

First, I don't know the specific professional field in which each reader is currently working. What I do know is that these concepts are universal and you will be able to apply them to your business development process with prospective and existing clients.

Second, I don't see any value in setting forth every concept and idea in the form of 'laws' or something rigid like that, since there are always exceptions to every rule. Haven't we seen enough books and articles that take that type of approach? While this book has the word 'guide' in the title, it is not an attempt to be the end all in the discussion of business development. The goal is to generate new ideas and discussions for you and your practice. The solutions that I share are intended to be open-ended rather than trying to be didactic or pedantic. In a world of 'click bait' and 'click holes,' I think that creating another book with a title like *The 12 Undeniable Principles for Building your Practice* or *The 8 Invisible Laws for Selling your Services* is too limiting and confining. Books with those kinds of titles are everywhere.

Third, this book has been written for the business development manager primarily, but its concepts and ideas can apply to anyone who wants to see their small- to mid-sized professional services firm succeed. This includes accountants, attorneys, insurance brokers, commercial real estate brokers and others, who currently work for a large professional services corporation.

This book is also focused mostly on professional services firms that specialize in business-to-business relationships, rather than selling to regular consumers. Many of the principles shared will help any professional services firm succeed, no matter if the target client is a commercial or private consumer. I have also done my best to zero in on helping the smaller firms that consist of two to 40 people, with a desire to keep things lean.

This book has truly been a labor of love for me. It was written from the perspective of someone who has travelled the long journey to success, not only as a business development representative, but also as a consultant and the owner of a professional services company. I have seen the ups and downs with each company and I have learned important lessons along the way.

I don't focus heavily technology or social media in these pages. There are plenty of books like that on the market. Technology is so ephemeral and in a constant state of change. This is a book about selling your services in a way that is real, easy-to-remember and most importantly, impactful. It's the most human aspect of selling.

Also, getting prospective clients through the door may not be your biggest problem. It might be getting them to commit to using your services and hiring you *after* they've walked through the door of your firm.

Don't let the title fool you. While this is an attempt to distill some complex ideas into something more basic and understandable, this little book is big on ideas and concepts for selling. The term 'bare bones' is geared toward getting down to the basics of these ideas and concepts without barraging you with too much marketing and sales jargon that isn't relevant to your profession.

I believe in the principles and processes I share in this book. I practice them every day. Most of the principles I write about are not new, nor revolutionary. So, as you turn the next page, I say 'thank you' for taking a chance on this book.

I'm hoping you'll find the following pages to contain not only practical information, but also ideas that will expand your mind and stimulate your thinking about business relationship development activities as they pertain to selling and marketing professional services to other businesses.

So, let's not waste any more time!
Read on!

Cameron M. Clark
June 2017

YOU!

As you may have already guessed, I don't have the secret to 'hack' your way to success in the professional services arena. You shouldn't manipulate your way into long-lasting, profitable relationships. That goes double for when you're working in the arena of business-to-business marketing and selling. This is the 'service' industry. In many ways, you aren't much different from those working in hospitality, retail and other fields, where the expectations from the customer are paramount. Likewise, professionals have high expectations from other professionals. It can sometimes be brutal. It's an ongoing, demanding process.

As a professional, you are in the business of serving your clients. You may be wondering how you can outsource that. If that's on your mind, then professional services might not be for you. Working in the arena of professional services isn't the same thing as selling a product like supplements online or drop shipping cell phone cases from some remote location overseas. It's a marathon, not a sprint. You can't work really hard setting up your practice for 3 years to reach the pinnacle of success and then decide you will outsource the hard stuff so that you can drop off the map halfway around the world.

It's the wrong kind of business for that kind of thinking. Perhaps you have been working in your chosen industry for a few years and have always entertained this fantasy, yet the results didn't come as quickly as you would have liked or at all. This isn't about selling gizmos or gadgets. This isn't about selling things. You're marketing and selling something else.

You are selling 'YOU!' That's right, Y-O-U. You are your product. You are your brand. You are the promise. What you have to offer might not be traditionally tangible. Your offering is based on the results you promise your clients.

Your product is *your* knowledge, *your* experience, *your* wisdom, *your* judgment, *your* commitment, *your* follow up and *your* desire to improve things for *your* client. It is all of the intangibles and some of the tangibles that make you the kind of professional that people want to hire. If you haven't figured that out yet or maybe you have forgotten it, it's time that you are reminded of that fact.

If you are non-responsive to prospective and existing client requests for information on a consistent basis or you are more focused on planning your next month-long, foreign vacation, you will fail. Time and time again, I have watched professional women and men achieve a certain modicum of success in their firm, only to flush it down the proverbial toilet by allowing distractions to take hold. These distractions might appear as longer vacations, later arrivals to work, three-hour lunches or personal drama that creeps in to their work schedule. It doesn't matter what industry these people have chosen to work in, this behavior is like a little hobgoblin that creeps in and sets up shop. After this little beast has made itself at home, only a superhuman effort to evict it from your head and habits will get the job done permanently.

There is no shortcut to get to the peak you wish to climb. I have watched more than one professional organization implode when the founder or founders stepped away prematurely to explore other business opportunities, retire or just 'find themselves.' Sometimes the business was salvageable, other times it was a wreck.

There may come a time, if you do things right, where stepping away from your business for a prolonged period of time and returning repeatedly, without seeing major disruption in the systems and processes you've established, could be a possibility. However, we're not there yet. If you're reading this book, it's because you see deficiencies in your current system.

My advice is to seriously commit yourself to the reality of your situation for now. If you're going to do this, commit to it for the long haul. I mean really, really commit. If you commit, it means you're going to be involved. Take in a nice deep breath, because you're going to dive in deeply and you're not coming up for air anytime soon.

Your desire to make things better for your clients should override your own comfort most of the time and it should be something you are conscientious about on a frequent and regular basis. If you are committed to the simultaneous cause of building your business while helping those clients who seek your help, you will wonder where the hours and the days went. You could even lose track of time.

Don't get me wrong. I'm not asking you to completely give up a life that happens outside of the company that you are trying to build or to grovel and let the client walk all over and control you, especially in situations where your professional advisement to the client runs counter to what he or she wants. Instead, I am merely suggesting that you have a service-oriented mindset when approaching the client's problems and the ways in which you might fix those problems.

Before we get to that though, let's get to know each other just a little better.

YOUR STORY

Since we've not met before you picked up this book, I have to draw a few conclusions about you and how I think you will benefit best from this book.

First, I think we can both agree you are a professional person with a lot of ambition. A professional is someone who gets paid for the specialized service he or she provides to other businesses or consumers. However, I think a more important attribute that defines a professional is the attitude and approach this person takes toward the work he or she is hired to perform.

Second, you may not be the owner of the company you work for, but instead you were hired to be the company's business development representative. That means you have been hired to be the lead facilitator in developing business relationships with prospective clients. This book applies to you too. Your firm may be big or small. Regardless of the size of your company, the ideas outlined in the following pages on business development will apply and will be useful.

Third, the traditional professional occupations you may be classified under could include attorney, CPA, commercial insurance broker, commercial real estate agent or some other professional who is working with other businesses every day. Less traditional, but still just as rigorous in its demands of professionalism are occupations like a court reporting agency proprietor, a payroll services specialist, a commercial property manager, a commercial landscape specialist or some other service provider. I am sure there are a number of 'hidden' industries that contract their services to other professional organizations that I don't list here. Those who belong to those industries will benefit from what follows. In nearly every case, you received specialized training for performing your work and how to get results, while not really ever being trained on how to sell those services.

Whether you went to college for your undergraduate, received a specialized, advanced degree for your profession or you started a professional services company straight out of high school, the one area absent in most educational forums was how to market and sell your services.

Some advanced degree courses may have covered parts of business development and the related tasks associated with building a specialized practice. It's likely the subject wasn't explored too deeply. The reasons for this kind of neglect are numerous and not worth the time to cover here. If you are picking up this book, it's because you feel your practice needs to grow and you are expecting information that will help you in achieving this objective.

MY STORY

I have graduated from a reputable university with honors and a Bachelor of Science degree in Communications. During my time in school and for a couple of years after, I worked in radio broadcasting as a morning radio show host.

After years of struggling to survive and raise a growing family on a radio personality's salary, it was time to move to a much larger city. I chose Las Vegas. I discovered business development almost by accident.

My first business development job in Las Vegas was with the oldest litigation support and court reporting company in the city. This firm limped along for years under poor management and even worse, nonexistent image management. Profits were the lowest they had been in years. I jumped in there as this small company's sole business development rep and began to experiment with basic ideas and sales concepts.

This experimentation on how to get commitments and build relationships paid off. In less than a year, gross profits for this tiny little company had grown from $90 000 per month to just over $200 000 per month! It was all because of basic ideas and concepts that I will be sharing with you shortly.

After a little over a year of working for that company and helping it get back on its feet, it was time to move on to new professional challenges that offered greater income opportunities.

My next place of employment was with a business I called my 'laboratory' for the next 10 years. I joined a tiny law firm that served homeowners associations throughout Nevada. At the time of my hiring, they were billing just over a half a million dollars in gross profits annually. Within less than five years, as the sole business development representative for this firm, we were billing more than 10 times the original amount. In other words, in less than five years, the law firm had gone from around an half a million dollars per year and just under a dozen employees to just over five million dollars in gross revenue and just over two dozen employees.

Again, I called that company the 'laboratory' because I was able to experiment with the business development ideas that I had learned from books along with coming up with my own ideas. Some were pretty effective and others were just plain dumb.

While I can't guarantee that you'll get the exact same results as I shared above, I can tell you that if you internalize these ideas and practice them daily, you will begin to see positive results.

Many times, while the competition was sleeker and sometimes manipulating their way into getting more clients, I just kept plugging away at improving our little company. It wasn't always hard work, but it was a continual level of attention to the work. It was consistent work, day in and day out.

Even now, I am still learning a lot. I have enjoyed much success over the years and I am excited to keep learning and growing in each environment I am in. The biggest lesson I've learned over the years is that if you put in an earnest effort and you're ready to learn, the opportunities are endless.

DEFINITIONS

It helps to have a clarification and common understanding of definitions so that we know we're all on the same page when we use the same terms:

Business Development
The activities associated with growing and strengthening the presence of a company in its chosen market through marketing, promotion, sales, strategic partnership formation or any other activity.

Marketing
Marketing is the activity of using various methods of promotion with the intent to sell a good or service in the open market to potential consumers. All of the marketing process is oriented to lead up to the sale.

Sales
These are the transactions that take place when goods or services are exchanged for money or

something of value given by the purchaser to the seller.

Remember, without sales transactions, the company ceases to exist.

Client

A client is a purchaser of a service or product from a professional service provider with the intention of forming a recurring business relationship based on the quality of the results.

This is a person, not a company. You build relationships with people, not the firm to which those people belong.

Always think of your clients as actual human beings, not things or just organizations.

Brand

The history of this word had to do burning some type of symbol into the skin of livestock to ensure that everyone in the area knew who owned the animal.

There are many ways this word has been defined. Some people mistake it for representing only the concept of a logo or some packaging for a product exclusively. Others see it as some intangible and therefore, almost indefinable quality for a company. This is also a mistake.

Your brand is not just the logo for your company or firm. It's not just some cute saying you put on the cover of all of your collateral marketing material. It's bigger than that. Quite simply, your brand is the complete package promise of results that you make to your existing and potential customers that extends from the copy you write on your website or printed marketing materials to the company logo you put on everything you give away to the way your receptionist answers the phone.

Bare Bones

The simplest definition of this phrase is that it is the essential or basic elements of a process or thing.

Nearly everything around us has a structure of some sort. Peel away the covering and you'll find a skeletal frame holding things up. Everything has a support structure, from the skeleton of a to the framework of a building. No matter how much muscle or brick or wood or steel comprises that structure, if there is no underlying framework in the form of dense material, there is no strength to stand.

Without an underlying framework or structure to the process you undertake, you will find regular weaknesses and inconsistencies in your business relationships, in the way you deliver your service and in the messages you are conveying. These weaknesses will undermine the very goals you are trying to accomplish. It is so important that you begin to adopt and ultimately master the basics of what I will be sharing with you so that you can become super adept at making changes in an instant when the circumstances permit.

What about all of the other complicated and crazy terms?

You may be longing to be dazzled by my knowledge of such terms as mindshare, a/b testing, growth hacking and all of the other popular concepts that have crept in over the years. Prepare to be disappointed.

Whether you love his work or couldn't care less for it, Ernest Hemingway is one of the most well regarded novelists of the 20th Century. Yet when you read his stories, you will find some of the simplest prose. Hemingway saw no benefit to using a long complicated word when something simpler would do. He knew his readers would 'get it.'

He elaborates some more in the following passage:

'A writer's style should be direct and personal, his imagery rich and earthy, and his words simple and vigorous. The greatest writers have the gift of brilliant brevity, are hard workers, diligent scholars and competent stylists.'

In short, the more complex you or I try to make something sound, the more we are moving away from being clearly understood. He even implies that it is harder work to be brief and direct than to be wordy and verbose.

In that spirit, I introduce you to my personal Bare Bones Philosophy.

MY BARE BONES PHILOSOPHY

I refer to the following as *my* bare bones philosophy, but really it's not something that is new. Minimalist thinking and philosophizing has become more common in our day of information overload and excess. Overall, I think this has been a good thing for most people as we become so easily distracted by the things needing our immediate attention.

I think you already have an idea of what a bare bones approach or philosophy might look like, so I won't belabor the point. In short, it is the mindset and practice of looking for ways to eliminate unnecessary processes, tools or distractions from your practice, while searching and implementing the highest priority activities into your practice. As martial arts star and philosopher Bruce Lee used to say, it is the 'stripping away' of the unnecessary to allow the best to come through. Adopting a bare bones philosophy allows you to move toward finding out what is working, then throwing out what doesn't work, thus giving you a chance to discover for yourself the things that are unique to your practice that can help you to be successful.

There are complex methodologies and processes that can always be implemented into your sales process, but most of the time, these resources can become a distraction. These methodologies can become a trap that makes it harder for you to be flexible, productive and capable in solving prospective client's problems. Taking a bare bones approach to business development will help you simplify your process, get results faster and keep your life and career from becoming too complicated.

The focus of this book is on getting clients. That's why you bought it. Getting clients means developing deeper and more meaningful relationships based on trust and a mutual understanding.

CUTTING CLOSE TO THE BONE - REJECTION

There are many books focused on teaching readers sales techniques that can help them be successful, while simultaneously ignoring the stark reality that the world can be a challenging and mean place. These books gloss over the reality of rejection as they claim to tell you the foolproof methods of overcoming rejections. These authors tell you that 'no' is really 'maybe' and all of that. Your reality is that there is no way to overcome *every* rejection from *every* person.

The truth is that rejection is a part of sales. Sometimes it might feel personal. It could even be intended to be personal. The best way to deal with this kind of rejection in a business setting is to never take it personal. Yes, it may in fact be a personal jab in one form or another against you and your firm when people turn you down. When you are tempted to get emotional about this kind of rejection, I invite you to memorize the wisdom of the Chinese philosopher Confucius:

'It is a fool who takes offense where offense was not intended, but it is an even greater fool who takes offense where offense <u>was</u> intended.'

In other words, no matter what happens, don't take things personal when you get rejected. It's going to happen. If you've never been in a sales situation where you are being rejected repeatedly, it can come as a shock at first. It can even lead to developing a cynical attitude. Guard against that tendency.

When selling professional services, whether going out and cold calling prospects or networking in a more 'warm' business development setting, you will be exposed to 'negative' experiences and 'positive' experiences. You will benefit most from viewing these experiences as just learning experiences.

Check yourself regularly as you perform your business development tasks throughout the day. Your attitude toward dealing with rejection, indifference and people avoiding you will determine much of the actions you need to take in developing your business.

To get over the fear of rejection, I tried to view the process like I was a player in a baseball game. I was the batter stepping up to home plate for a chance to hit the ball. This was the same thing as putting myself in front of the prospective client and facing possible rejection.

The more opportunities I gave myself 'at bat,' the more possibilities were available for me to make a sale and get the commitment to do business with the prospect. I was continually active in the process without taking myself too seriously.

Keep in mind that you can 'step up to the plate' hundreds of times, but if you don't have a process in place to move cold prospects to warm relationships, you might get a couple of lucky hits at best. With a well-thought out process for approaching prospective clients and working to build productive, profitable relationships, you may increase that percentage from single digits to upwards of 20 to 30 percent. Who knows? Eventually, you might be batting .500. It's a matter of focus, planning and consistency.

Just remember, being rejected is a part of business. It doesn't matter what business you are in, not everyone is going to want to buy your services. The key is to get through as many of those who are ready to reject you as quickly as you can, so that you can find the ones who do want to do business with you.

BETTER COMMUNICATION BASICS

Clients come in all shapes and sizes. They have diverse religious, cultural, ethnic and economic backgrounds. If you're doing your job right in business development, you will see that kind of variety on your client list. Regardless of the demographic cross section of your current client portfolio, just remember that any successful client relationship stands the best chance of success when all parties start things off on the right foot. The key is to make this step intentional in the beginning stage of your business relationship.

This is not a new idea, but it is certainly not used in enough professional situations. It's about zeroing in on the tone of communication you are engaging in, along with the channel through which the message is transmitted to your clients. It also helps to examine how they seem to want to communicate with you.

It is one thing to communicate. Everyone can communicate. The problem is that not enough people know how to communicate effectively. Much of the reason for this is that they haven't explored the factors affecting their communication, as much as they have studied the content of the communication itself.

In other words, you need to engage in communication about how to engage in future communications. This is beyond just sending the message itself. Instead we are discussing the ways that you can both send and receive the messages more effectively.

This process is called meta-communication.

Meta-communication

Social scientist Gregory Bateson is one of the first researchers in our modern-day to discuss the following concept. Originally, it was intended to only apply to the nonverbal cues and related actions and tones connected to a verbal conversation. Over time, it has evolved to encompass all of the signals and implications related to communication between at least two parties. However, the term may go much further back than 20th Century social science.

To the ancient Greeks, the prefix *meta-* meant 'beyond.' This word was used for a few different things: like metaphysics and metamorphosis. In our day, we use it for terms and processes like metadata, meta-emotion, meta-memory, meta-humor and so on. To borrow a metaphor from Dr. Stephen R. Covey, if we are applying the prefix *meta-* to certain concepts means that we are going to take time to examine the lens we are using rather than continuing to look through the lens itself.

The word 'communication' generally refers to the two-way exchange of messages between parties. So, meta-communication is moving beyond this two-way exchange or stepping outside of the process and examining it for what it is, not just what it is saying. It looks at the way the message travels. It's the way that we set up that framework to enable open and clear dialogue with those with whom we are trying to communicate. In other words, it's the process of communicating about communication.

How does this apply to burgeoning client relationships?

I first came upon the process of meta-communication while working with a client years ago. There were instances when this client had dealt with some challenges that one or more of my subordinates had created for her and her company. Rather than just giving up on us and switching to a competitor, she would reach out to me to discuss the problems we had created. A number of times, she would call me just to process what was on her mind. Other times, she was looking for a solution.

At the beginning of these kinds of conversations, she would say something like: 'I need to talk to you about my concerns and I just need you to listen to me for a few minutes. I need you to keep an open mind and let me talk. That way I can get what is on my mind out, without interruption and we can discuss it afterward.'

Imagine the damage this could have done to my ego. The first time or two we had this kind of conversation, I remember the desire to want fight back and resist over the phone with my own criticisms of the way things were going over at her company. It's not as though they were perfect either. Instead, I held my tongue and I would listen and take notes on what she was saying.

Every time we did this, it was like a light had gone off to reveal some aspect in our company that we needed to improve or change. After those discussions, I would take my notes and share them with the key folks in my company so that we could develop solutions to her problems.

Over time, as we had more of these conversations, they became shorter and shorter. It wasn't necessarily because there were fewer problems or we were coming up with the solutions more quickly. I believe it was because she and I had begun to understand each other's shorthand in meta-communication; so communicating became easier for us.

So where were the meta-communication techniques in that example? It was in her setting up the framework for our conversation before we'd actually had it. It was in her asking me to allow her to communicate a certain way so that she could get her message across. It was also in our conscious awareness that meta-communication was taking place. Ironically, if you had asked her to define the term 'meta-communication,' she may have been hard pressed to answer.

There are other ways to approach the discussion about meta-communication with your client. You'll know the best way to do it. By the way, you don't have to use the term 'meta-communication' when discussing preferred communication methods. It's probably best not to. This could lead to more confusion for the client. Sometimes it's best to just say something simple like: 'I wanted to take a few minutes to discuss the most effective ways we can communicate with each other.' Usually that will be an effective way to get the ball rolling.

You may dismiss this as idea as fluff and time-consuming by saying that you will know how best to communicate with the client through instinct, but I guarantee that if you use these ideas, you'll never miss your mark. Regardless, I think communicating about communicating might be one of the keys to your firm's success. There is so much potential gain for you to create a smooth working relationship between the client and yourself.

I started using this technique from time to time with other clients, both prospective and existing. When a new relationship was developing between prospective client and myself, it was invaluable to know what ways he or she would want to be communicated with on a regular basis. Sometimes, it was clear that there was one method for communication that the prospective client could not stand and other times it was them expressing which method or methods he or she preferred.

Finding out which communication methods the prospective client preferred early on helped create a deeper level of trust faster since they would be receiving the information in their preferred channel every time. I was making the deliberate choice. I would also communicate this information to those assisting me at the firm to work on the prospective-turned-existing client's business. You can find out with a statement as simple as:

For instance, Ms. Jones may have complained about the way her accounts were serviced by the previous provider and that she was a bit annoyed with their constant use of email. The conversation you have with her after or even during your initial consultation when she has expressed interest in your services could go something like this:

'Ms. Jones, as we've discussed in past conversations, you had mentioned that you were not a big fan of email. You felt that it was sometimes unclear what your service provider was trying to communicate to you. What are some of your preferred methods of communication instead?'

This facilitates a simple, yet easy-to-implement insight for you and your firm that will lead to better relationships of trust. Once the client relationship was in full swing these techniques still came in handy. For instance, when a client would call or visit with me, it became easier to spot the anger or frustration the client had with the situation.

In those times, I would usually allow the initial rant to come out from the client. Many times it was a sort of ramble that had the potential to go on in a sort of chaotic fashion for longer than necessary. To guard against this tendency, when they were taking a proverbial breath, I would insert an acknowledgement of their feelings and then try to redirect the conversation toward something more productive and constructive. Asking questions usually accomplished this best.

An example of this kind of attempt would go something like this:

'It sounds like there are a number of things that are a concern to you. I am sorry to hear we haven't been performing up to your expectations in that area. I have a suggestion. What I have found is the quickest and most valuable way for us to improve on a client's concerns is to allow the client to lay them out for me, <u>without me interrupting</u>, except to ask a question here and there. Afterward, we can see if there are a few things that can be addressed in the call and whatever I can't find a solution to now, I will work on it afterward and let you know the results. How does that sound?'

Without fail, the client calmed down and agreed to have that kind of conversation. After all, what did he have to lose? In many cases, it was fun to see the client taken aback by this approach. After all, in today's society and especially, in professional services, it is expected that the service provider will feel slighted and will fight back and get defensive.

The above example that I shared is not defensive. It isn't about groveling either. It's about acknowledging something is wrong and then moving forward with the client to find a solution.

Applying these meta-communication practices to business development, it can be something as simple as asking the prospective client about preferred communication channels and times of the day when it would be best to communicate. Make sure you take notes about these preferences. It's also helpful to note to yourself whether the prospective client is a direct communicator who is to the point or more of a talker, who likes long conversations. After you've determined their preferred communication style, you will be able to better communicate with the client effectively.

As the service provider, you are the one in control. Or at least, you *should* be the one in control. Meta-communication techniques like the one I shared above can assist you in staying in control of your own emotional response. However, being in control doesn't necessarily mean having all of the control. There is a difference. You can't control how the client will react. You can't control the way they will feel or think. You can't change them. Nor should you try. I've watched too many service providers ruin perfectly productive client relationships, because they couldn't stay in control of themselves in those times of crisis, stress and conflict. This was usually because they were trying to control their clients' actions.

Managing Expectations

It is important that you know what the client expects as clearly as possible <u>before</u> you begin doing business together. It is almost as important for the client to understand what you can realistically deliver. Once they set those expectations, it is vital that you meet those expectations every time. The client is looking for a certain level of predictability. The more predictable you become, the greater level of trust your client will put into you and your services. If you fail to meet those expectations after a long track record of delivering on what the client is asking for, it is likely you will be more easily forgiven than if you start out the relationship with unfulfilled expectations.

Tying that back to client communications for a moment, what about mitigating potential problems such as missed calls, delayed email responses, etc? I have seen so many times when service-based companies make promises of returned phone calls within 24 hours or answers to all emails within a certain amount of time and then they fail in their attempt to fulfill that promise. This promise can come in the form of the outgoing voicemail greeting or an out of office reply in your email. Most of us add in these promises, without even thinking about it. If you don't think you can do it, don't promise it. At best, it will be seen as a tactic intended to manipulate the prospective client into doing business with you; at worst, the client will take it as you being completely disingenuous and they will spread the story of your poor service delivery around town.

I think it never hurts to be upfront with the clients and prospective clients on this situation. Unless you have an iron-clad system in place to return calls and emails without fail, acknowledging that you sometimes may need time to look into issues or gather information could take longer than 12 hours or 24 hours or whatever you promise. If this is the case, be sure to communicate that with the client with a quick call or email in advance. If possible, be sure to mention to the prospective client during the initial business development period that this is how you will operate. This is meta-communication.

It does you little good to make the assumption that clients will automatically know it will take you a longer time than usual to solve their problem. Most of the time, they will respect your honesty. Put yourself in the shoes of the client for a moment. If she sends you an email inquiry and doesn't hear back from you, for a couple of days, yet she expects a reply. She doesn't know that you're busy working on solving her problem. At that moment, her perception is her reality. It will be your reality too.

The sooner you understand not only what you need to communicate to your client and vice versa, but also the most effective ways to communicate with your client, the better the outcome for all parties involved in the relationship.

Communication Preferences

So, what is the easiest way to determine preferred communication channels between you and the prospective client?

Ask them. You could ask questions like:

- *'What is your preferred method of communication? Phone/Email/Letter/Face-to-Face/Text/Other?'*

- *'What times of the day is it best to communicate with you?'*

- *'What are you looking for in the way of results and the reporting of results? Status Reports or Profit & Loss Statements/Summaries/Etc?'*

- *'Do you like to be presented with numerous options for action, a select few or just the best recommendation based on our firm's assessment of the situation?'*

Once you've collected this information, it is vital you keep it all in one place and reference it regularly. If you have software or some sort of shared drive that helps manage this information, use it. However, you may want to take a low-tech approach and keep it all in a book or binder. Whatever, the case, it should be easily searchable and easily accessible.

The information should not sit idle either. Put it to good use. Your clients will be appreciative of the respect that you show when you communicate with them in the manner they prefer. In the next chapter, we'll talk about how to move the prospective client from being a prospective user of your services to an existing client.

BETTER COLD CALLING

Not everyone who reads this section will be placed in a situation or a market or an industry that requires the actual process of reaching out to a prospective client. If you have been hired to develop business for your professional services firm, then it is very likely you will be calling on these prospective clients regularly. At some point, you have had meet each prospective client for the first time. Referrals are always going to be the most effective way to get business. However, there are never enough referrals to replace the need for a cold call. The following ideas and tips are a collection of things I have learned, studied and used over the years to build business relationships from scratch and therefore, create more profits.

The phrases 'cold call' and 'cold calling' can evoke various emotional reactions from different people. Most of the time, the emotions are negative. It might have to do with portrayals of sleazy, slick, silver-tongued salesmen portrayed in pop culture over the years. From Willy Loman of the classic Arthur Miller play 'Death of a Salesman' to the desperate salesmen who were fighting for their jobs in the play-turned-film 'Glengarry Glen Ross' to the numerous incarnations of the pushy sales rep in so many movies and television shows. The stereotype I think of immediately is the character of Herb Tarlek on the classic late 70s TV show 'WKRP in Cincinnati.'

Tarlek was a plaid jacket-wearing, polyester pants-sporting, bribe-taking advertising sales manager for the ailing AM radio station. Slick talking and a bit lecherous, Tarlek did no favors in creating a negative impression professional salespeople had to deal with in 1970s America.

I think that portrayals of salespeople like Tarlek and Loman might be part of the reason why so many professionals shy away from learning sales skills until they start to feel desperate. They don't want to be seen like a sleazy sales guy or gal.

It's time to get over this aversion. The sooner you get over it, the sooner you will succeed.

The Mindset

So what is the mindset for cold calling - Bare Bones Style? In some ways, it is practical to adopt what Sun-Tzu called the 'Death-Ground' strategy.

One example of this strategy is to think of yourself as an ancient warrior who came over to the coast of a strange new land you are about to invade with your army. Your leader would order your ship be burned. As you watched the glowing embers of the once magnificent ship, you are told that you now only have two options: die with honor fighting on the battlefield or defeat the nation you had come to conquer and take control of that land.

Like the ancient warrior, you also must attack your work with reckless abandon and the desire to succeed and win. Once you step off the ship and set foot on solid ground, you must be determined to not look back or look for retreat. Thankfully, you won't lose your life in professional sales, but it is this determination that will help you succeed.

The Process

Do yourself a favor.

Forget about cold calling as just the same as selling. If you think of it as selling, it could cause more anxiety than necessary to get the job done. Instead, think of it as getting commitments. This is not about closing deals. Even when you get the final commitment, stop thinking of this as 'closing' a deal.

Regardless, each time you contact a prospective client, you should have some end goal in mind. What is your ultimate purpose for contacting them? For example, it's important that you work toward getting a commitment, even if it is something as simple as getting permission to send some more information via email, to attend a seminar you will be presenting in a couple of days or to allow you to make a follow up phone call next week. Getting them to commit to you in the process will be a key ingredient to your success.

Cold calling is really a simple matter of introducing yourself in a friendly, non-pushy manner to the prospect and greeting them with respect and a genuine interest in getting to know the client much better.

Timeless Tips

There are a few things to keep in mind when approaching a prospect for the first time.

First, unless you get their permission to use their first name, it's best to address them as 'Mr.', 'Mrs.' or 'Ms.' Addressing the prospect or client this way might seem formal, even in business for the 21st Century, but formality like this can go a long way. You will appear respectful and you might even stand out in the eyes of the prospect when you first meet them.

Second, remember to smile here and there, but make sure it appears genuine and feels real to you. The last thing you want is to seem like a phony when you are attempting to connect with another human being. One of the things that can help you when smiling is to make sure your eyes are reflecting your smile too. Often, when we're faking an expression, it can become subliminally apparent to the recipient that we are faking by noticing that the area around our eyes doesn't reflect the smile on our mouth.

Third, be authentic in getting to know the person. However, don't spend time pretending to care about things that the prospect is interested in, but you have no desire to discuss or learn about. That will come off as insincere. It's good to take an interest in what they are interested in and what they are doing, but it doesn't mean you should have to fake your interest in those things. Sometimes, it is enough to be interested in the fact that they're interested.

Finally, if there is something you can bring into the office like an edible treat, coffee or something useful that reflects your company's brand, then bring it with you. You know that your strategy is working and that the item you dropped off was a good one when the prospective (and existing clients) begin to associate you with the item you dropped off. It happened to me on multiple occasions and it led to higher profits.

The Approach

Whether it's on the phone or in the prospective client's actual office, asking to speak with them is your first step. Remember to be nice to the gatekeepers. They literally control your access. Even if they turn you away the first couple of times, just keep being polite and persistent. I have won so many accounts by returning again and again intermittently over the course of months and months to places that seemed impenetrable at first.

I never felt bad or any kind of negative emotion about their lack of interest in my services at first. My approach was a bit laid back, but always friendly. I never pushed or prodded. I was convinced that the business was one day going to flow toward my company and it did!

Your approach on the phone for a cold call shouldn't be too different. Once you get the prospective client on the phone, don't get overly excited, but acknowledge you are happy to be speaking with them. Hopefully, they will reflect a similar enthusiasm. If not, don't let that get you down. Continue to appear and sound enthusiastic. A warm smile will help in creating this impression.

Also, while I would discourage following a full-on written script, it doesn't hurt to write down some of the things you will want to say in the call. It also is good to write down what your goal is for the call before you start dialing.

When I have made many of these calls in the past, whether it was in person or on the phone, it usually followed a pattern of my greeting them with a brief introduction, some background on my organization and the reason for my visit. The prospect may then begin the conversation with basically one of three responses: a) a full out rejection of further communication, b) some skepticism in the form of a question that may or may not be based on something you've already stated or c) a comment encouraging you to continue to share more information.

I shared these three outcomes in the order of most likely to happen to the least likely, as has been my experience. Many times, you will find the prospect unwilling to continue a conversation about your services or even lack of willingness to disclose anything about their company's current situation. Just roll with it. If you do receive a skeptical remark or question, take courage. This is a part of the business building process.

The average cold call should be geared toward one goal and that is to get a commitment from the prospective client. I don't necessarily mean a commitment such as just 'closing a sale.' Rather, it is a commitment to let you send over some information via email (that you will be able to follow up on via phone in a couple days) or a commitment for the prospect to log onto your website and take a look around at some new demonstration you might have added or it could even be inviting them to lunch in the next couple of weeks to discuss things further. All of these are valuable steps in the right direction in the unpredictable and sometimes seemingly messy road of business development.

Remember, this is just an introductory greeting to the prospective client. You are not some door-to-door sales representative who has to close a deal by the end of the day or you won't get a chance to eat. This is a process that can take some time and patience. Getting to the next commitment is vital in this process.

The Client's Challenging Questions

In a cold call situation, you may be caught off-guard by a challenging question from the prospective client with whom you are speaking. We all end up in this situation. The reasons for this kind of open challenge from the prospective client can vary from some negative experience they had before with your firm or even more simply, something negative they heard about your firm. The questions the prospective client asks might be difficult to answer or even worse, be something we don't know the answer to or can't remember. Sometimes, the natural inclination is to start talking more in the hopes of stumbling across the answer. Other times, you might be tempted to 'dance' around the answer to the question without really answering it altogether. I've also seen times when the preferred method is to change the subject.

When you are confronted by this kind of challenge, there will be times when you don't know the answer. It's okay. A simple: 'I'm not sure how to answer that. Can I look up some information on it and get back to you by the end of the day tomorrow?' may suffice. Other times, you just need to buy a little time. In those situations, I highly recommend that you respond to the question with a question of your own. Respond with questions like:

'What are some of the reasons that your employees are finding that software difficult to use?'

'Have you experienced that slow response a lot in the past from other suppliers?'

'How often has this been happening?'

You might even have to pull out the very simple question:

'I'm curious as to why you might mention that concern. Can you tell me more about it?'

Yes, I am aware that some of the questions are close-ended and some are open-ended. In this scenario it likely won't matter too much as the prospect senses the question is an invitation to speak more. If they say 'yes' when you invite them to tell you about a concern, they will naturally flow into the reasons for bringing it up.

This gives you a moment to think about what is being said, but it also gives the person asking the question a moment to think as well. There isn't just this continual stream of information that the two parties are trying to blast at each other. Just make sure you are listening for feedback and input from the prospect with whom you are speaking. This will come in the form of answers to your questions. Also, make sure that they have a chance to ask you more questions. The more questions they ask, the better, even if they don't seem convinced you are the right choice at that moment.

Know When to Fold 'Em

I've hinted about this above in a few different places, but often, you will find the cold call is just not going your way. That's fine. If the prospect is losing interest in talking to you or the prospect seems distracted or he is beginning to send signals that he is not interested in pursuing any further discussion with you, respectfully wrap up the conversation and get out of there…for now. If it's on the phone, do the same with a polite, courteous and concise statement. Something simple like:

'I know you're busy and have a number of tasks to get to today, so I'll let you go and maybe check back another time.'

'I respect your time and I am sure you have a loaded schedule, so it might make sense for me to let you go for now and maybe check back in a few days. How does that sound?'

To the diehard, old school salespeople of yesteryear, this likely appears to be heresy. Even if you aren't old school, it might seem counter-intuitive. Just remember, this is not the last time you have to fight this battle with the prospect. There will be other opportunities. You afford yourself those opportunities when you leave the prospective client with a good impression.

What those old school guys and gals might have a hard time acknowledging is that their hard-driving tactics and desire to close a sale on the spot have made people in business simultaneously more jaded and more savvy than ever before on hard-driving 'tactics.' These days most prospects will spot that kind of manipulation and pressure from a long way off.

Regardless, I think that your own confidence in your services will sometimes shine through much more clearly when you are willing to vacate the prospect's premises early. It's best to have a sort of strategic withdrawal the first few times rather than to persist in the hope that they will begin to like you the longer you stay.

MBWA

Management consultant, Tom Peters, used to talk quite a bit about the concept he'd developed called: Managing By Wandering Around. I remember reading about it when I was already practicing a variation of this approach as a business development manager for my first professional services firm that handled litigation support services. After I read what he'd said I adapted and modified my approach to: Marketing By Wandering Around. .

The opportunity to use this concept may come after a number of follow up calls to the prospective client's office. Rarely does a prospective client allow immediate access for the business development representative they haven't vetted. Be patient. Remember what we discussed about treats and other goodies.

Anyway, you will use MBWA if you get through the front door, preferably with a treat or some sort of useful item as we'd discussed earlier, and you will want to meet as many of the decision-makers (and those who can influence the decision-makers) as possible. This will involve wandering the halls of whatever office building you are in and greeting many of these prospects. This has probably been one of the greatest and simplest (not to mention most affordable) things I've ever done to build business.

Quite simply, it's another way of getting to know people as you move through the office, taking mental notes on their professional and personal likes and dislikes and forming the beginning of relationships with them that are cordial and friendly. Sometimes, someone who is not directly connected to the department you are seeking business from will be able to assist you by passing along vital information and resources.

After you finish visiting with the prospective client(s), be sure to drop a thank you card in the mail or at least send a brief thank you email. It can go a long way.

One last parting tip on this concept that goes for literally everything in this book: stay off of your phone. For being an inanimate object, a smart device can be quite demanding of attention. When your phone dings, beeps, rings or buzzes while visiting with the prospective (or existing) client, resist the urge to check it and see who it is. It doesn't even matter if you tell the prospect that you are expecting a call or a text. It's bad etiquette.

8 BARE BONES TRAITS FOR BUSINESS DEVELOPMENT

Too often, in society and in business, it seems we're so focused on the differences between us that take for granted the things we have in common.

The following is not a complete or fully comprehensive list of qualities that a service provider should have to be a successful business developer. These eight concepts will likely to lead you and your practice to greater success than you may have ever seen in the past. It's up to you to make the decision whether or not you want to use them.

What follows is an examination of the essential attributes of: Humility, Enjoyment, Desire, Organization, Confidence, Commitment, Perseverance and Flexibility.

1. Humility

You've seen it time and time again, the wunderkind who invents a new product, turns in a spectacular performance or strikes it big on the Internet, becomes an overnight success and is then lionized by the press and is heralded by his peers as a genius or prodigy. Sometimes, it's the young artist, musician, inventor, athlete or performer who is showered with awards. More locally, it might be the young attorney who was given a partnership in a family practice before he had met the same requirements for other partners in order to become a partner. It could be the insurance broker who got into selling the right lines of insurance just as the market took an uptick demanding more of that type of insurance.

What do many of these examples have in common? For the most part, they didn't start out as a part of some grand scheme. If you had asked these travelers during a low point in their journey whether or not they knew fully what they were doing, nearly every single one would have said 'no.' There was no grand plan or scheme to bring about their success. For the most part, it was about being the right person at the right place in the right time and just working on their craft a little at a time, every single day.

However, the story doesn't end there for most people. When success is achieved, there can be a tendency for the successful person to feel as though he or she has 'arrived.' There is a desire to start rewriting the story of how success was attained, leaving out some of the negative parts. This helps create a more flattering perception. Nassim Nicholas Taleb calls this practice the 'narrative fallacy' and he considers it a dangerous practice.

These successful types fly closer and closer to the sun and their waxwings begin to melt like the legendary Icarus, but they don't see or sense it until it is too late. The feelings of mastery, entitlement and being exceptional begin to creep in. Hubris. It is at this moment that the fall from 'greatness' may have begun. It's not an irreversible descent, but most professionals never see it coming until it is too late.

You may think I'm only talking about arrogance or cockiness, but if it were only that, the problem could be remedied within a relatively short amount of time. It's subtler than that. It's the little things, the distractions that begin to move into the territory of your mind to pull you away from the day-to-day habits and practices that helped you become successful. The little things you did daily to achieve success don't seem relevant anymore. You tell yourself that you're on a different level than before and so now it's important to keep moving up to the next level.

Another lie is that you have surpassed your peers and sometimes, your mentors. Your mind tells you to eliminate the basics. You may tell yourself to focus on the big picture and the little stuff will take care of itself. That's the loop that you'll be tempted to play in your mind over and over again. Why go through some of the mundane, when the exciting is right in front of you and is sure to stay with you forever?

Or is it?

It's easy to excuse yourself. You might tell yourself that you're different now: If you achieve your goals and you have a successful career, that you will not be seduced by taking the easy way. The easy way may be not returning calls in a timely manner or at all. It might come in the form of not being as courteous in your email responses or when meeting with clients. It might even just be not showing up as often to the office. You could be telling yourself that you are the exception.

However, you are anything but the exception.

Writer and journalist Andreas Kluth wrote about this temptation when speaking of successful C-level executives and their desire to give into the temptation:

'One academic study examined corporate bosses who became successful and famous, and found that they subsequently spent disproportionate amounts of time writing their memoirs, giving speeches, and joining boards of other companies. Perhaps most tellingly, their average handicap on the golf course fell from 15 to 13 after they became famous. Meanwhile, their companies began failing.'

2. Enthusiasm

Have you ever met a person who seems bored with life? They lack energy or the interest to want to engage with the people and environment around them. How long have you wanted to spend time with a person like that?

Many clients bring a certain enthusiasm or at least a deep personal concern to the table when they approach a professional services provider to solve their problem for them. If the professional service provider doesn't reflect that energy of the prospective or existing client or if the professional just appears to be ambivalent about working with the prospective client, it can have negative repercussions.

In writing this, I am reminded of numerous instances where I would need to hire an accountant or meet with an insurance broker about an issue or problem that I needed solved. In some of these initial meetings, there was an obvious lack of energy, connection and overall interest from the professional in what I was bringing to the table, which was basically my money in exchange for services. Needless to say, they rarely got hired if they were low energy and low enthusiasm.

I've sometimes heard professionals say this instead: 'I can tell in advance that the client and I won't be a good fit. Rather than saying I'm not interested in working with them, I thought being indifferent to their problem was an easier fit.' In those cases, you are actually making the problem much worse. The prospective client's interest in using you and your services wanes and he or she doesn't just go away. This person will go away telling others what a flake you are or worse, that you're incompetent and uncaring. They will share their experience with others and leave a negative impression with them as well. I won't even bother mentioning the social media and online review sites that will reflect the negative impression you deliver.

If you are a business development representative for a professional services firm and you notice a lack of enthusiasm in one or more of the professionals you are supposed to be selling for, do your best to encourage them to show a little more energy. Sometimes, it's an uphill battle, but it's worth the effort.

Meeting the commitments you make to your clients, whether its reviewing or rewriting a draft for a letter they want you to send or returning a phone call or attending a meeting when they request it, these are the things that go a long way in building trust with your client. Know that your ability to follow through on the things you say you are going to do with the necessary energy and vigor required will be one of your biggest assets in building your business.

3. Desire

Desire, specifically the desire to learn, is a close cousin to enthusiasm.

Generally, when there is a lack of understanding or progress in learning, we associate it with those of an older generation. In turn, they appear unenthusiastic about the learning process. However, in my years as a manager, business owner, teacher, parent and consultant, I have seen that it isn't just that subset of society that struggles with learning new things. It's members of every generation, so the problem doesn't have to do with age.

Whether it was learning a new application on their smart device or learning how to become more effective in dealing with other people, these people were often resistant and it felt like the process took that much longer. I've shown employees who worked at my company simple software functions that they'd had no desire to learn prior to their need to use them. Once there was a need to solve the problem, they became much more invested in the process of understanding how to use those systems and functions. The desire was always there inside them, they just needed a catalyst and context for activating it. I believe the lack of desire to learn new things holds more people back than they realize.

If a professional has a low desire to learn something new whether it is as basic as spell checking her emails before sending them or as complex as developing a comprehensive quarterly financial report that analyzes five different departments' way of spending, the problem is still the same. It could be as simple as returning a call from a prospective client on the firm's services. If she doesn't find the desire to do certain things, she will struggle in completing those tasks.

The desire to learn may make or break you, no matter where you sit on the spectrum of success. I know there are other factors that can slow the progress to understanding something new. These obstacles can seem very real. These obstacles can be overcome with time, modern breakthroughs in understanding cognition and the learning process and a consistent effort. I believe if you can create desire from within yourself to learn something new, then the learning process becomes easier.

I've only spent time on how cultivating the trait of desire in your life and profession can help you learn new things, but there is also great power in just having the desire to succeed. Desire is what can lead to setting and achieving your financial and professional objectives. This desire manifests itself in wanting to create results for your clients. Desiring to do an excellent job for your clients and keep fulfilling the commitments you make to keep and build more trust is key to your success.

Search yourself and see if desire is in there. It really can be the fuel that will propel you and your business to the next level of achievement.

4. Organization

You may have tried to get organized before. You might have attempted to set up multiple organization and time management systems meant to create more simplicity with folders or note cards or apps or whatever. After a few weeks (or just days in some cases) of attempting to keep up with this system, you discover you just can't do it. You can't keep up. This is natural and not something you should allow to affect you going forward.

You could be in another camp never really attempting any kind of system of organization for time and project management. You might feel its best to fly by the seat of your pants and let things happen naturally. Many times, this can lead to days or weeks where one urgent task follows another and they seem to pile on top of each other so deeply that it begins to feel like you must devote 24 hours straight to getting everything done and even then, it still will not all be done.

It is usually better to be organized than to 'wing it.' Conversely, you should avoid becoming so rigid in your scheduling or filling your day with so many projects that you lose sight of the simple joys in life. Ultimately, it's up to you to find the solution and that balance. I don't think there is any time management system that rules over all of the others, since each individual has a different background and a different profession than the next person. Therefore, the needs of each individual will be different.

It's also about knowing when to eliminate unnecessary tasks or projects. It's about priorities. This is something I've struggled with in the past and still have to work on from time to time. It's hard to say 'no' to certain things you know you should be turning down. It can be difficult to delegate and let go of certain tasks or even entire projects. Keep things simple. Don't turn a simple process into a long ordeal that requires everything to be filled out in triplicate.

It can be a tough thing to ask what you must do to simplify your projects, your schedule and your methods for running your practice. It requires difficult, but necessary introspection and a desire to learn what matters most and what can be eliminated or delegated to others. When you are able to assess these things honestly with the mindset to simplify your approach, you will find deeper satisfaction and focus on the things that you are attempting to do and that you will accomplish.

5. Confidence

We've all seen what a little confidence can do for a person. When someone has their head slouched and their shoulders leaning forward, it can be an outward indicator of more than just poor posture. It can indicate that that person, whether man or woman, does not believe in themselves or what they have to say. It's a profound truth that people trust and believe those who trust and believe in themselves.

I remember my first shift on the radio. I'd been working behind-the-scenes with the station for a few months. It was nerve-wracking to record my first full four-hour shift on the pop music station.

My voice was shaky at times and I'm sure my intonation was awkward. However, I endured and I persisted. I really tried to improve. Each shift that passed was a better shift than the last. I think a lot of this improvement was tied into how conscious I was of my self-image. The less I focused on myself, the better I seemed to be doing. I really began to let go of the feelings connected to anxiety over what other people would think about me. I also released my irrational desire for perfection.

It wasn't until years later as a professional business development manager giving professional presentations for groups, large and small, that I started to really 'get over myself.' If you truly want to show confidence, you have to stop worrying about what other people think about you and stop worrying about the outcome of each interaction with another person.

However, getting over being self-conscious is only part of the solution.

Next time you are in an encounter with someone, whether over the phone or in person, pay attention to how you are holding yourself:

- Are your shoulders back?
- Is your back straight?
- Are you remembering to smile from time to time?
- Do you look the other person in the eyes when you speak to them?
- Do your hands stay in your pockets the whole time or behind your back? Or are you using your hands for dynamic, energetic gestures?

Now examine your mind:

- What are you thinking?
- Are you paying attention to what is being said?
- Do you go into conversations or other social encounters with others playing a dialogue that is primarily negative and self-defeating?

If there are moments that you notice that little hobgoblin of self-doubt creeping into your mind, cast it out with reminders that you *do* belong where you are and that you *are* competent and able to assist the person you are addressing.

If you place your focus on serving others and you are looking for ways to help those people, everything else takes care of itself. You begin to forget about what you look or sound like or whatever weaknesses and insecurities you perceive in yourself.

It may seem contradictory that I just gave you areas to focus on to improve your confidence and then followed it with the recommendation that you focus on others, but it makes sense. This helps prevent confidence from transforming into arrogance or overconfidence. No one really enjoys spending time around someone who is cocky. A healthy, daily dose of quiet humility that reminds you that you are no more special than anyone else with whom you work, will keep that in line.

If you are sincere and the kind of person that others can connect with on a deeper level, you will have no struggle in presenting an image of confidence and self-assuredness. Caring about others in a genuine manner shines through in most interactions. This will definitely make you more attractive to the potential clients with whom you would like to work and it will lead to more business than you can handle.

6. Commitment

Have you ever worked for an organization or a company where the leaders appeared distant or would just disappear for a long time without explanation?

These founders would just up and leave in the middle of the day and make themselves completely unavailable to assist with answers to your questions and other issues. I've seen this behavior in many organizations and it's a recipe for a drop in employee morale and less new business among other things.

Whether it could be attributed to a case of feeling overwhelmed or 'burnt out,' this drop in visibility is a lack of involvement and therefore a lack of commitment. If you've read this book from the beginning, you will notice this has been my theme on almost every page. I am asking you to invite your clients to make commitments to you and your firm. In return, you must commit to them that you will get the job done and get it done right.

Dr. Stephen R. Covey once said:

'Without involvement, there is no commitment. Mark it down, asterisk it, circle it, underline it. No involvement, no commitment.'

I really like what Dr. Covey is saying here. Put another way, you could say:

'The higher your level of involvement, the higher you show your level of commitment. Mark it down, asterisk it, circle it and underline it. Higher involvement equals higher commitment.'

Even more simply: *Higher involvement equals higher commitment.*

The more you immerse yourself in a project for work, a hobby or something else, the more you become committed to that project. There are numerous world and historical figures that immersed themselves so deeply in their cause that it became difficult to differentiate between the two.

Mother Teresa was a Catholic nun who dove deep into the work of helping those who couldn't help themselves in Calcutta, India and other places around the world. Her name is synonymous with this kind of charity. No doubt she was involved and therefore deeply committed.

Sir Winston Churchill faced numerous defeats earlier in his political career moving through the leadership ranks in Great Britain. As catastrophic world events unfolded around him and his nation, there came a moment in history where he was undoubtedly the right man for the job and despite the physical dangers and hardship, he stuck to his post and helped the British isle survive German bombings in World War II.

Dr. Martin Luther King Jr. led oppressed men and women in the United States of America to greater civil rights and freedom. It was a long haul for the reverend and there is no doubt he was committed. In the end, his life was taken from him for his involvement in one of the greatest movements in American history.

Setback after setback wouldn't derail entertainment mogul Walt Disney. Hard to believe, but his first company went bankrupt before he had achieved the success we associate with him so easily today. In those days, a bankruptcy could have ended most entrepreneurs, no matter what industry they worked in. However, he was committed. His involvement in the industry of animation and entertainment was born out of an obvious love for creating new things and telling stories.

The good news is that as you ponder the above examples, no one is asking you to move to India and help the poor or to run for public office or to have to swim the murky waters of financial insolvency, nor would you be required to give up your life for your cause. However, the lesson that can be taken from these four people and numerous others is that they immersed themselves in the work they were doing. They didn't stop and as a result, they became some of the most impactful individuals the world ever knew.

Even though these people achieved amazing victories and saw world-changing results in their lifetimes, they didn't stop. There was never a case of 'burn out' or the need to completely 'go off of the grid.' Remember what we discussed at the beginning of the book? YOU are your greatest product for your professional services firm. It is important YOU are committed to it and to your clients. Take time to rest and recover, no doubt. Just remember that YOU have made commitments and as a result, YOU have got to get involved again. It's a perfect circle.

7. Perseverance

The message has been clear many times and in many places: Don't give up. Never, ever, ever give up. So many have said this time and time again. From leaders like Winston Churchill and Vince Lombardi to more current influencers like Brian Tracy and Steven Pressfield, there really is a theme that you must persevere until the task is done. Most sources define perseverance as pursuing a course of action with steadfast determination, even in the face of difficult odds.

When I was a business development representative for the local collection company, there was a company with prospective clients whose personnel had been extremely loyal to another collection company for a very long time. The connection between the two companies was so strong that I was once told it was as though the employees between these two companies had a psychic link. Every few weeks, I would drop in and continue to talk with the many managers there who I thought would one day decide to give our services a try. Following each visit, I would email those managers and thank them for their time and interest in the company.

I never gave up and my perseverance paid off.

The opportunity came almost two years after I'd made first contact with some of the managers in that company. The company was going through an ownership transition and the managers with whom I'd been meeting were now the ones who had some control over where business referrals would go. They wanted to give our company a try to see what we could do. They weren't upset at the other company or anything, but wanted to see what kind of results we could produce.

From then on, more and more business began flowing our way from that company. I was grateful for the business. I never stopped my visits following all of this new business. I feel that the effort to win that business had been worth it and I did my best never to take it for granted. Along the way, problems would creep up and we would work on solutions together. Every time, all parties walked away satisfied with the results.

It wasn't until nearly a year into our business relationship with each other, that one of the key managers who'd been instrumental in getting new accounts to come our way, confessed to me how sorry she felt every time I came into their office in those early years. She was certain there was no way our office would ever get the business as our competitor had locked things down with them. She said that giving us a try was just a token way of letting us know they'd appreciated the time I'd spent in their office talking to them and working on solutions to their problems. It was the results that we'd produced early on that led her to know we were serious about what we did and making things happen for her and her team.

8. Flexibility

When you are flexible in your professional and personal relationships, it doesn't mean you are a pushover. On the contrary, you are usually more skilled at getting what you want or most of what you want over the competitor, who can be the proverbial 'stick in the mud' about certain areas of compromise, like price and negotiation. The reason for this is that you are able to communicate your needs better than the rigid individual who is unable and unwilling to see the other side of the issue. Those types of people usually flex *back* rather than flex *with* the changes requested of them.

Furthermore, flexibility doesn't always mean losing battles to win wars. Many times, the flexible individual will avoid combat from the start, because their minds are open to various possibilities and they aren't so emotionally connected to the thing they want so badly that they risk destroying the relationship. They aren't in a defensive mode.

The flexible professional is able to spot potential areas of conflict from a long distance and they usually can mitigate much of this prior to it getting out of hand. One of the keys is to take your ego *out* of the equation rather than inserting it *into* the situation, as many professionals are apt to do. Appearing more important than you are or like the most knowledgeable person in the room can have negative consequences.

Take assessment of yourself in this area. Do you go into most discussions, whether personal or professional, with the intent to win? What does victory look like? Have you defined it? Is it an end goal or is it the means to an end? In negotiations, what is your goal? To convince the other side that you are right? Is it to get everything you can out of the other party? In other words, are you trying to conquer the other party? Are you speaking more than listening? Do you find most of your interactions to be negative?

Regardless, flexibility is an area we all can work on. I find myself having to check what my interactions are like with others professionally and personally all of the time. I'm not perfect at it. Nearly every day in my profession, I am working with different types of personalities, who come from different backgrounds and are all interested in different things. Sooner or later, conflict will arise. Remember, conflict is not necessarily a negative thing.

The key is to not to lose your head in those situations. Instead you must be willing to sit still, listen and really try to pay attention to what these different parties want. You do this with the intent of hopefully getting it for them, as long as it's in their best interest and within the law.

You've worked hard to develop the above traits, but where do you go from here? How about a practical application of all of these positive character traits into a pattern or system that makes it easier for you to make the connection to the prospective clients you want to do business with and ultimately get their commitments?

GETTING COMMITMENTS

What if we stopped using the phrase: 'close the deal' or 'close the sale?' Using the word *close* in reference to the sales process is that it implies finality. To close something means to make it come to an end. In turn, it feels like all of the attempts to make a good impression and to persuade the prospective client have ended when we say we 'closed the sale.' There's a disingenuous feel to these phrases. It's subtle, but its also possible that continual use of this phrase in your firm might lead to an attitude of complacency once the client has signed on the dotted line.

This way of thinking is a dangerous trap. However, if we all knew it was a trap, there would be much less client turnover at most professional firms. Where the problem lies is partly in seeing the selling process as a bunch of parts rather than a connected process. In the traditional approach to sales, there can be a fixation on 'stages' or 'phases.' It is an attempt to break something so simple and natural as developing relationships that could ultimately become friendships into parts and pieces. This can sometimes lead to rigid methodologies and ideas that can convolute something so simple as business between two people.

Instead, the selling process should be seen as one 'eternal round,' like a ring. To me, selling has always been about getting commitments while developing a solid relationship to do business together. There are so many places along the way that you can be extending invitations and getting commitments from the client. That's what I want to share with you. It might be the most important thing you take away from this book.

The following pattern is something I was taught many years ago. Its application was actually used for another purpose, but it really was so valuable and useful that I began incorporating it into my day-to-day life as a sales professional. Over time, I have modified it and added to it. My whole goal in every change that I made was to create a more genuine aspect to the process, so that the desire to go for the hard, fast 'close' wasn't a concern. This was because the relationships I established would be strong enough and so full of trust that doing business would be easy and smooth. This pattern is simple to learn and easy to incorporate into your daily business-building routine. Practice these ideas and you'll see fast changes.

These ideas can work in nearly every professional services business development situation. As we progress through this process, please pay attention to how we are building, brick-by-brick, a firm foundation for a future business relationship of trust with our prospective client.

Do not take the following ideas lightly. These are very real principles when it comes to human relationships. More importantly, the following process is effective for developing trust between two or more parties.

We are What We Do

Much has been written about habits. In short, if you're developing positive habits, it will enhance your life and your practice. Likewise, if you are developing negative habits, they will diminish what you are trying to accomplish. Imagining that you can stay in neutral in your own personal and professional development, while expecting the business to thrive around you is a delusion.

The following process is something that I have used in thousands of professional business development situations that led to powerful profitable and lasting results for my business and many other businesses where I have consulted. I'm sure you've used many of these ideas as well.

The first goal you should have in mind when you meet someone with whom you would like to do business is to develop a functional level of trust. Often, this starts with the skill of 'small talk.'

Small Talk

In just about every new encounter, this is the first thing that happens in many conversations. It can be at a party, an industry event or when you drop by the prospective client's office. In these situations, it is important that you maintain a professional demeanor;

especially if this is the first time you are meeting the prospective client.

To many, small talk skills may seem easy to take for granted. However, try imagining a scenario in the past where you were engaged in small talk with a prospective client and you could barely remember a word she said about her life or her family or even her occupation. You may even have had trouble remembering her name. You were so focused on what you would say when the time came to present a proposal for your services. It probably felt natural to be preoccupied with the desire to do business with her. The problem comes when that sole focus overrides the genuine desire to get to know her as a person.

This is why small talk is an excellent tool to use in nearly every encounter. It should allow you an opportunity to get to know the client better and to develop a level of trust with her that will be mutual between you and therefore, more likely allow you two to do business together. There are at least two reasons why this would be important.

The first is that it allows you to build on common beliefs with the client. You want to find some things that you agree on. It's human nature that people who are able to agree on some of the same things usually will get along better than those with opposing beliefs or those who are under the impression that they have opposing beliefs. Like attracts like.

The old adage to stay away from discussing religion and politics still applies in the 21st Century. In fact, you may be pious or you may be political, but your allegiance to certain things irrelevant to business can be a turn off to some prospective clients if you spring your personal beliefs on them.

Before you think I'm telling you to avoid 'being yourself' or changing who you are so that you can get the business, let me clarify. If you plan to do business with a prospective client, what *you* will talk about is primarily under *your* control until *you* enter one of those two controversial arenas. I know of a few instances where a client decided not to do business with a professional service provider, because they learned early on where that professional stood on a political issue and the client wasn't a big fan of that stance. On a side personal note, I had a client once make the switch from using my company to another, because he had learned what my private spiritual beliefs were through another source. It hurt for a moment, but I never let that stop me from being polite and professional toward him.

Before you say that the above examples are the kinds of people you don't want to do business with anyway, just remember that we all have enough in common that we can get along with just about anyone professionally. You have the power to determine whether or not your conversations will devolve into some sort of religious or political discussion. In some cases, this can actually be a positive, but only after you have established and built a foundation of trust and understanding with the prospective client that is solid and clear. It can happen.

In my years of developing professional relationships, I have oft been surprised by the diversity of people with whom I've developed relationships. I have worked with clients who'd belonged to a range of political and religious groups. I've done business with atheists, devout Christians, practicing Muslims and orthodox Jews; all while many of them had no idea what personal religious beliefs I held. I didn't hide them; they just never asked. It wasn't important that I made my personal religious beliefs known to them. That's not why they hired me. If someone asked about my spiritual beliefs, I would tell them what I believed without embarrassment, apology or hesitation, but I didn't dwell on it and usually, they didn't either. However, when it came to politics, I cultivated a generally apartisan attitude that has allowed me to be friends with Republicans, Democrats, Communists and Libertarians and any other political faction. When the subject matter veered toward the political realm, I would try to steer the conversation back to something more substantive. This skill becomes doubly important when you are hosting group gatherings and one or more of the people in the group start talking politics. Even if you agree with the instigator's point of view, this can be deadly ground. It could lead to hurt feelings and isolation of one or more of the group's other members.

There is a solution to guard you from this temptation. You can be the best version of yourself by taking a deep interest in the other person. Every time you find the prospective client asking you a question about yourself, feel free to share something briefly, but redirect that question or another like it back to the client. Think of yourself as a mirror reflecting back the parts of the person that they like best. Do these things enough times and you'll find the client will be bonding with you much more quickly than if you continued to talk only about yourself.

During the small talk process, you may be asking the prospective client about her family, her favorite pastime or how she spent her weekend. Remember to pay attention and be a good listener. This is her life and what's important to her.

The second reason for the necessity of small talk is that diving right into 'shop talk' with a person you barely know can be viewed as opportunistic and tacky. It can also feel like a shock to the prospective client where she is assailed with statements or questions about business the moment she sat down.

There are relationships that will develop in this process that might require more small talk at the beginning, but after multiple meetings, the small talk will be sprinkled throughout the conversation, as you both attend to the business at hand.

There will be occasional times when you will be instructed to dispense with the small talk and get to the main point. Some people just give off the vibe that they only want to talk business with you. Be ready for that. Don't take it personally. Just be ready to 'talk shop' with these types of people, when and if they want to talk shop. Regardless, the more you focus on developing this skill, the better you will become at navigating it.

Remember that each time you encounter a new potential client you are starting from ground zero with that person. Leave the hang-ups and baggage you may have developed dealing with other prospects at the door. Sure, it's possible that these new prospective clients may have heard about your firm and your shortcomings. That is a head start and it is a good thing, even if the prospective client tells you something negative she's heard or perceived about your company. This gives you a chance to clarify and correct those misconceptions about your company. The key is to keep the conversation moving forward toward a greater level of trust.

Exploration Questions

This is where the real work gets done. This is the one tool that you will and can consistently call upon throughout the process at any given time. It's also one of the only elements under your complete control at all times. I can't tell you how many times that I have been in a sales situation that was requiring a greater level of trust and by asking the right question, I helped move the process forward. Other times, I have been met head on with a conflict that was so visceral from an employee or client that you could taste it. The only way I was able to save myself was by asking questions. The environment and their demeanor were sometimes so hostile that I felt the only defense was to ask more questions.

Essentially, there are two types of exploration questions: Closed-Ended and Open-Ended Questions. Both are valuable and knowing when to ask which type of question is an invaluable skill.

Close-ended questions are usually defined as having a 'yes' or 'no' answer. They can also involve getting a quick, fact-based answer like a quantity or some other fact. Some examples include:

'Would you like to take some information about our company?'

'Who is the best person to talk to in your company regarding your current insurance policy?'

'How many full-time employees does your firm currently have in its employ?'

'Do you feel there is need for improvement in our services?'

I think closed-ended questions sometimes get dismissed a little too easily in communication circles. The questions themselves can be valuable when asked at the right time. Where the problem usually occurs is when you start asking a succession of closed-ended questions in a row to the point that it starts to sound like an interrogation. The key to making close-ended questions work for you is to know when to balance them with open-ended questions.

Open-ended questions are usually designed to expand on information given previously in the closed-ended question process. They usually have a more subjective tone than closed-ended questions. Sometimes they reflect feelings or opinions, other times it might be something to do with getting clarification on some matter.

Some examples of open-ended questions can include:

'What are the three top priorities you're looking for in a professional service provider that you're not getting now?'

'What are your thoughts about our online status alert service?'

'When do you think you and the board of directors will be meeting to decide on the proposal we discussed last month?'

'I sense you have concerns about this new service. If so, what are they?'

These questions can be powerful. Used in conjunction with closed-ended questions, they can be an effective method for developing the trust-based relationship you are seeking and they can build it quickly. Showing true, genuine interest in the person or people you're talking to will be enhanced with this kind of questioning.

Taking Notes
When I managed a team of over twenty employees, I used to reference an old Chinese proverb: 'The faintest ink is more powerful than the strongest memory.'

Sometimes, in the face-to-face meetings you have with prospective clients, it helps to take written notes. If you decide to take notes, always do it in analog fashion with a pen and paper. Typing notes on your phone, tablet or laptop is a distraction and will lead the person speaking to you to feel as though you are not really listening. Taking notes during these kinds of conversations has three advantages.

First, the person speaking to you will feel more comfortable opening up to you, because you outwardly appear to be listening. One way to check this comfort level is to ask the speaker if it is okay that you are taking notes. Almost every time, it is guaranteed to be okay.

The second reason taking notes can work in your favor is quite simply for the sake of easy recall. Think of how long and protracted some prospective client relationships can be at times. It's nice to be able to recall the notes you took in the past from a conversation that may have happened weeks or even months ago.

A last reason is that it can help slow the conversation down to where the pace is under your control. If there have been negative feelings expressed, it gives you a chance to change things up to where you might be able to lighten the mood. When someone hostile toward you or your firm sees that you are taking notes, it shows that person that you are someone who cares enough to take the time to listen.

Building Consensus

This can be vitally important in the initial stages of a burgeoning relationship with a prospective client. That is to find out if there are other parties with whom you should speak. Some examples of these types of situations include the possibility of the prospective client needing to check with a spouse, business partner or life partner before moving forward with a decision.

Better to get that kind of clarity before you launch into a long dialogue you might have to repeat later. In larger group settings, where you may be relying on multiple people to make the decision to choose your company, the sooner you can engage with multiple decision-makers, the more likely you will be successful in getting new business.

This may be a blind spot for you and your company. The more parties get involved on a decision-making process, the more convoluted it can become. You can't control who is involved in the decision-making process, nor can you control how many people are involved. What is under your control is your ability to find out how many people will be involved and who they are, so that you can work to tailor your message to their preferences.

Presenting your Bare Bones Message

Though I will be using the word *present* to discuss the conveyance of your message to the client, I want you to think of this more like a discussion. Yes, you will likely be doing much of the talking at the outset. That's natural at the beginning of any presentation. However, if you can see this as a discussion rather than just you delivering a long string of unbroken sentences, your ability to connect to the prospective client will be augmented tenfold.

Going through the exploration questions with the prospective client gives you the ability to tailor your message in the best way that meets their expectations of service. If you gloss over asking good, in-depth questions early in the exploration process, you will be making a potentially fatal error.

Believe me when I say there is nothing more disconcerting than to have prepared a presentation only to discover during the presentation that a new concern has popped up. This is often because one or more of the key decision-makers wasn't available during your initial exploration phase. Remember to ask good questions.

Keep in mind that this isn't a pitch. A pitch is something you throw. The pitch is a relic of the old-time ad men of Madison Avenue who had to get a client emotionally excited about an idea that they had conjured and then decided was in the client's best interest. That's not what this is about. You aren't pitching your message; you are *discussing* it.

The framework for presenting your message can take more than one format. Some presentations are as casual as possible with you sitting across from the prospective client in a small office and the air conditioning isn't working. Even less formal is a conversation on the golf course.

Other presentations might be more formal with you standing before a large group of people in a fancy room, flanked by one or two team members, working to convey your competence and skill. Some might be done on the phone or in videoconference. Then there are the ones you will do from your desk when the prospective client drops in unexpectedly. All of these need your undivided focus and attention.

The most powerful factors that will influence how each presentation is delivered will be the setting you are working in and the length of time you have been given. In other words, it is important to be flexible and to prepare to be flexible when you are presenting your message.

In small business settings where your firm is trying to sell to another business, it does you little good to follow a rigid format in presenting. Even worse is the reliance upon a software program to make your presentation like PowerPoint or Keynote or some other audiovisual crutch in the presentation. Never turn to these software programs or anything like them in a sales presentation. If you must use them at all, do so sparingly. These software programs have a place in training and education, albeit sparingly, but rarely ever do they enhance a sales presentation. There are plenty of presenters over the years that fell on their own swords accidentally by relying too heavily on their tech dazzling everyone.

Remember, you want the prospective client to connect with you. You are the product. Also, in line with the bare bones philosophy, you should always lean toward the simpler, less complicated means for presenting your message.

Going back to the framework for your presentation, it is important that you have some sort of overarching message you are trying to convey. The more concisely and succinctly you are able to distill your main message into only a few sentences, the more effectively it will come across to the receiver and the greater the intended impact. Often, it will be tempting to go really long and perform a 'data dump' on the prospective client. To you, it will seem like you are dazzling them with so many facts and figures that tie into your extensive knowledge. It will be tempting to try and convince them you are an expert in your industry. The way they see this approach will likely not be the same as the way you see it. More often than not, delivering a seemingly long and unbroken string of facts and figures rarely impresses anyone and it certainly will not lead to a connection with the prospective client.

My most frequent and usually most successful approach was when I worked to engage the prospect in a bit of a back-and-forth dialogue about their business and current situation early in the discussion. In some cases, it was making a couple of quick and concise statements about the meeting we were having (meta-communication) and then asking some questions about what problems they were having. Sometimes it helps to warm up the prospect by starting with some fact-based questions that will lead to short answers like revenue projections for the coming year or the names of key decision-makers in the process. This can warm up the 'mental muscles' of the prospect to give you deeper and more meaningful answers later in the discussion.

I have given presentations to three people and also to hundreds of people in another room, sometimes in the same day. Some factors such as tone and cadence of voice along with your facial expressions should never change, whereas the volume of your voice and some of your gestures might need to be modified. You don't have to have a big smile plastered across your face the whole time, but being aware by showing a friendly countenance is valuable.

Your speaking voice should veer away from the monotone and into a more buoyant timber. You don't have to sound like a radio DJ or some big arena announcer in any type of presentation. Instead, work to be conversational in your tone. The goal is to try and make each recipient feel as though you are connecting with them and them alone. That's hard to do in a large room, but it can be done with practice and experience. You will hope that they will take away at least one or two valuable items of information.

Speaking of takeaways, it is good to have something to give away that is informational and useful to the client. The key is to have something that enhances your presentation, but not replaces it. In other words, if you are practically reading from the document you will be handing out, you will cause a few attendees to wonder about the point of listening to your presentation in the first place. Many times, I will hold off on handing out material until it is absolutely necessary. This usually comes at the end. My reasoning for that is that people have very limited attention spans. It only takes one minor distraction to take the focus off of what you are saying and then place it on someone or something else. If you or an assistant are handing out folders about your service or some white paper on the topic, wait until after you have delivered an impactful key point. After that point has been delivered, handing the item to the attendees will be more effective since there is a context now for them to understand the document you've just given them.

Clarifying and Resolving Issues

After you've presented your message, there will likely be questions and concerns from the client. It is better to invite these questions from the client instead of waiting until they spring up later in the presentation or somewhere further down the sales process.

Use the context of your presentation with the questions and comments that were happening during the presentation. It's best to start with the right context and then ask an open-ended question that invites an open-ended answer.

From time to time, you may get an emotional response from one or more of the attendees. It might have been something you said or something they read in the material that you shared. It might have been some bias or problem that arrived with them to the presentation. Often, these kinds of responses can be quite visceral. When you are faced with that kind of emotional response, it is vital that you keep your cool. It's not you they are attacking, its almost always the idea or concept. When this happens, keep asking questions. It is better to work to clarify an issue before jumping in with a solution. This attempt to understand the prospect's concern is valuable in establishing an outward, genuine desire to solve the problem.

I've had many times when I said something that triggered an emotional response by one or more of the message recipients during my presentation. To regain my footing and composure, I have found temporary refuge in asking additional questions. These kinds of emotional responses from the client were almost always because the person receiving it misunderstood something I'd tried to convey either through my speech or in our collateral material. There were also times when I might not have conveyed the information as clearly as I had originally thought. As I mentioned a moment ago, this helped to show the person asking the questions that I wanted to understand them. Most of the time, this led to them calming down and returning back to a sense of normalcy in the meeting.

Communicating ideas and concepts, all while trying to build a real connection with a prospective client is a challenging process not unlike an uphill climb. Once you learn how to do it, it becomes more rewarding than anything else you could imagine in business.

The Invitation

As I've mentioned, the sales process is ultimately about getting prospective clients to make commitments to use and pay for your services. All along the way, you are making commitments to them as well. This ensures that there is a connection and it is real. Getting commitments is what all of this is about and hopefully you will make it into a regular habit.

Sometimes, all you need is a simple invitation to the prospect to get them to do business with you. Years ago, one of my business partners observed a key difference between how he had built his firm prior to my joining the business and then how I built his business in subsequent years. He'd said that he felt we were both effective at getting to know the prospective client better and really understanding his or her needs. He also observed that we both seemed to outline solutions and communicate those solutions to the prospect effectively. However, that's where the similarities ended.

He'd said that when he'd get to the end of a meeting or would leave after a presentation, he hadn't really defined nor expressed what he wanted the prospective client to do next. Frequently, he'd left out the request to get the prospective client to take the next step. He'd left out the invitation to do business together.

As a result, his message became muddled and his intentions were not so clear. He said he'd sometimes leave meetings thinking: 'Well, I hope they liked the presentation. At least, I felt good about it.' I'm sure they liked him, as he was a very likable guy.

However, the phone didn't ring as often as he probably might have liked. Many times, the business was going elsewhere.

Does this experience sound familiar? Have you given what you felt was an informative presentation, yet, there's still something lacking? I'm going to share with you some of the things that I did to ensure my presentations weren't given in vain.

The difference my business partner had noticed was that I appeared fearless in *asking* the prospective client for the business. In other words, he knew I would get the necessary commitments most of the time, because I had made it clear that I was seeking them. Everyone in the room knew why I was there and what my intention was in talking to them. I was bold in asking or inviting people to come to our side of the table when the time was right to make the request, while still maintaining a friendly, cordial atmosphere.

I reflected on what he said repeatedly. The difference might have been that I was simply extending invitations all along the way and then getting minor commitments from the prospective client. After getting those commitments, I would follow up. This trait was not inherent in my DNA or personality makeup. I wasn't always good at extending invitations and getting commitments. It took a lot of practice. It still does take a lot of practice.

When I have gone into invitation and commitment situations, I have tried to maintain the mindset that I literally had nothing to lose if we don't get the deal. To get to this point, I had to say to myself that it wasn't the end of the world if we didn't move this forward. Each commitment had been a small step in the right direction. It was about starting small and getting the little commitments, not the big ones.

The other part of my mindset was telling myself that we'd built a company that was performing a service in our market more perfectly and operating more in the best interest of the client than nearly every competitor in the market at the time. My hope was that this interest in the clients and what would help them best would be conveyed in my words, actions and other signals to the prospect. With those kinds of thoughts in mind, I went in with confidence. There was no feeling of desperation in most of my meetings with prospective clients. Much of that was due to the mental trick I outlined above.

People can smell desperation. They can tell when you're anxious and nervous. They can also sense confidence and self-assuredness. Trying to get 'closes' from the client is often a seller-focused approach and if things go wrong, your desperation will become obvious. Closing deals and trying to get the prospective client to say 'yes' over and over runs the risk of being seen as applying negative and undue pressure. It can be seen as pushy and quota-focused, rather than doing what is in the best interest of the client.

Getting commitments is client-focused. It is open-ended and allows the client to feel like they have a choice in the matter, which they always do. Taking that kind of thinking a step further, when you are focused on getting commitments, it is likely you are also willing to make some commitments of your own. If the prospective client is unwilling to commit, you just keep the conversation going to see what is standing in the way. As a result, you will never become frustrated or discouraged and as a result, desperation will not show through, because you will never feel it.

I remember the late radio talk show host, Jerry Doyle telling the story of how after making a comfortable living in New York as a stockbroker how he wanted to become a Hollywood actor. Doyle moved to Los Angeles to try his hand at acting by going to audition after audition. Of course, he went through the same rejections that other aspiring actors and actresses went through. I'm sure at times it was humiliating and embarrassing. However, he went into an acting audition and within a matter of minutes he finally had to stop abruptly. He turned to the casting agents who'd been watching his performance and half-jokingly asked them for a paper towel.

Naturally, the casting agents were confused as to why this unknown actor would cut short his performance and do such a thing. To paraphrase Doyle: 'Because the audition I just turned in was about the same as dropping a deuce on your floor.'

He said that he walked out of the room knowing he wasn't going to get the part. However, he knew something more important and that was that he'd maintained his dignity.

Doyle's irate manager called the next day. He blasted Doyle for pulling such a risky and stupid stunt. After blowing off some steam, Doyle's manager finally told him: 'they want you to come back tomorrow and audition for a different part. You were different from all of the other actors. They liked your genuine approach.'

Doyle went on to become one of the lead actors in the TV series *Babylon 5*. He would watch auditions of struggling actors and actresses who would come in to read for bit parts on the show. More often than not, he said many of the men and women smelled of desperation the moment they walked into the room. He said that it was easy to see which aspiring performers were attaching all of their hopes to each audition and which were not. Those who seemed desperate were the ones who rarely got the jobs.

Now, I'm not recommending that you make some joke about going to the bathroom on the floor or anything. What I am recommending is that you adopt *some* of the swagger and mindset of Mr. Doyle. Having that swagger gives you the feeling of dignity and it commands a little more respect. It's important that this swagger is always balanced with some humility. Remember that people are attracted to and want to do business with those who appear self-assured and confident. This includes the process of extending invitations and getting commitments.

If you stammer or you hem and haw around the issue of getting the client to sign a contract, you unintentionally convey your lack of confidence in what you are selling. You show a lack of confidence in yourself. Remember what you are selling.

Y-O-U!

You'd better be confident in your product and you'd better show the prospective client your confidence in your product. The secret to gaining that confidence and showing it doesn't start with the things you say or how you stand (though those things are very important). It has to do with your focus on delivering solutions to the client. I'll share more with you on that later.

That's what the essence of a bare bones approach to getting a commitment should be like. It's actually as simple as saying 'Great! Now that we've gone over the particulars, *will you* take a look at the agreement and sign it today so that we can get started?'

See how easy that was? Remember, to get a solid commitment out of someone, you need to ask him or her to make the commitment at some point in the process. It's not always done in the same way every time, nor is it done the same way for every prospective client. Sometimes you have to do it repeatedly and in creative ways. What better way to begin a request than to start with the words 'will you?' Try these:

'Jim, I see you have some more questions. One of our contract supervisors is in town next week. Will you join us for lunch on Friday and she can answer more of your questions?'

'I appreciate your input, Mr. Ching. I appreciate your interest in the seminar next week. Will you ask your regional managers if they could attend as well?'

To some, this might seem a bit forward and abrupt. However, let's try looking at it a different way. If someone has no interest in using your services or anything else, even after getting to know you and your company better, why waste much more time trying to 'prime' them for moving forward? If you've laid the groundwork and you've been preparing them with the above concepts, then it makes sense to move this relationship to the next level.

Also did you notice how each of those requests began with a 'will you' and not a 'can you' or 'could you?' While the alternatives like 'could you' or 'would you' are possible in getting the commitments you might be looking for, 'will you' seems to have the right mix of direct command and polite request attached to it. When you boil it all down, it is just another simple question. It's a question with a purpose.

So, taking this further, if it were for business development purposes, you might try something like this:

'Now that we've looked over all of the paperwork, do you have any questions? If not, will you sign it and authorize us to move forward?'

'Shannon, I appreciated your time this afternoon. You'd mentioned that you wanted to bring your colleague, Ramona in on this discussion before making a final decision. Will you ask her what days work best and invite her over for another discussion?'

'I know we covered a lot of material, Santiago. My hope is that you've received enough information to make an informed decision. Feel free to take the items I've shared with you today and share them with your partners. If they like it or they don't, will you call me and let me know of your final decision?'

When you request a commitment, it is vital that you pause after you make the request. Let them answer. Sometimes it can feel a little uncomfortable and awkward in that silence. Become comfortable in that moment of pausing. They will respond, even if it feels like its taking 20 minutes. It will never really take 20 minutes to get a response, but you must be the one who is in control or at least appear to be in control of the situation.

You may get a 'no' or a 'not really.' Be respectful of that answer. However, take courage in the fact that 'not really' sometimes means 'not right now.' It's also possible the discussion might need to continue. This brings us back around to something I touched on earlier with you.

Know When to Stop

One final insight that I think it vital to your success in nearly every sales situation you encounter while working to get commitments is to know when to stop selling. Too often, I've seen the strong invitation extended and answered with a powerful, resolute commitment from the client, only to be weakened by a lingering on the scene by the seller.

The same goes for those prospective clients who continually rebuff your requests to proceed. The last thing you want them to walk away thinking is that you are pushy. If that happens, you have effectively killed the sales process.

Follow Up Questions

Asking more questions and hopefully uncovering and then resolving other concerns are a vital part of this connection process. If you are able to pull back each time and allow the prospective client to speak, you will discover a number of things that might help you to help them.

This kind of strategy can help you uncover what might be bothering the client. Regardless, it is always important to keep your cool, breath evenly and not take anything personally when people say 'no.' Sometimes it isn't the right time to do business yet, but being able to ask a few more questions after trying to get a commitment and close the deal might get you there.

Overview

What I have attempted to share with you is a very simple and stripped down attempt to make the selling process more productive. All of these steps have led to one thing: Connecting with the client so that when you invite them to make a commitment, they will want to do business with you. All along the way, you are working on getting mini-commitments. Keep going, you'll get blocked sometimes or diverted, but remember, the process is about getting commitments.

Master these ideas and you'll be on your way.

THE BARE BONES DON'TS TO ATTRACT NEW BUSINESS

The next few pages will discuss the simple, mostly practical methods that work and don't work to attract new business. We will start with things to avoid doing when marketing your small professional services firm to other businesses. You may have been tempted to try some of these in the past or even done a few yourself. Avoiding these in your business-to-business professional marketing strategy will help you save time and money:

General Phone Directories
It happens every so often. A well-meaning sales representative from one of the remaining phone book publishing companies in your area will drop by your office and tell you how much she can grow your business by advertising in a general area directory.

The first problem with the rep's statement is that electronic media such as search engines, local business review websites, mobile mapping software and other social media are replacing this once well-used resource. Some of this problem for local print directories has been mitigated as many local yellow page publishers are taking their business online. Through some SEO (search engine optimization) implementation on their part, these area directories and other locally published directories are still able to keep things going.

The second problem is that these directories never get updated. Every year, when one shows up on my doorstep, I have randomly paged through it for a couple minutes. Inevitably, I would see businesses where I'd worked locally five or ten years ago were still listed, but with some out-of-date detail such as an old address or the wrong name for the firm. Doesn't this tell you something? If they don't even bother to update the simple listing there, why would they spend a lot of time caring about your half page listing in the directory?

The third and most important concern to consider is that you are pulling from a limited prospective client base. If a sales representative from one of these paper directory publishers comes into your office and is trying to sell you on advertising with their book, I don't care how pretty she is or how handsome and charming he might be, you must know that they don't really understand your business. You will waste your dollars on their publication. The only exception is if you also have a service that you also offer to the general public. Even then, it may be a bit of a risk.

I remember numerous occasions where a sales representative came into my office attempting to convince me that advertising through their general directory made a lot of sense for my professional services firm. They didn't take time to research my business. We were solely focused on our business-to-business market, which consisted of less than 1000 professional individuals in the state. Why would I give them money?

Radio & Television Advertising

Unlike the area directories, I see radio and television advertising continuing as an advertising fixture for quite a while. Terrestrial radio has survived the advent and proliferation of satellite and Internet radio along with podcasts and mobile music devices the same way broadcast television weathered the rise of satellite and cable service providers years before.

The problem isn't that it can't be or wouldn't be effective. The problem is that it might not be right for you and your professional services firm. As a business-to-business professional services provider, your market is limited. Why spend valuable dollars on advertising that is likely going to only be meant for less than 1% of the population? Remember its called 'broadcasting' for a reason. Broadcasting is basically 'throwing' (casting) your information to the general (broad) public in the hopes that a few inquiring souls will follow up on it through the myriad of information coming at them. It's just not effective.

One quick caveat I should mention is that broadcast advertising can be effective for business-to-consumer services. The local restaurant that is putting something new on the menu or car dealerships that slash prices will almost always benefit from broadcast advertising. I think there is definitely still a place for it, just not with your business-to-business professional service. Don't let a well-intentioned account executive with the local radio station or television station tell you otherwise.

Billboards

Hopefully, you're starting to see a trend here. So far, everything that I have shared with you involves something that is big, broad and impersonal. There is no point in using this form of marketing unless you are also servicing a business-to-consumer market with your firm.

I will add to this movie theater advertising. It's a trend in various pockets of the United States and Canada to have local businesses advertise on movie screens to the general public before the movie starts. The key word in that previous sentence was 'general.' If you were only looking to establish relationships with 3000 to 5000 prospective clients (individuals) in a market of a million people, why would you waste time and money on movie screens and billboards?

Newspaper Advertising

Newspapers once ruled the day. Now everything is going digital. It's not as though newspapers in their traditional paper form aren't ever useful or informative, but who are we are trying to reach? If an accountant only targets and specializes in working with corporations of a certain size or with nonprofit organizations, there is little likelihood that advertising in the newspaper is going to boost their business with those types of clients.

One caveat is when you are asked to write an article in the area in which you specialize as a professional. Nothing beats that kind of established credibility and ultimately free advertising in the form of exposure to a broader local market.

General Magazine Advertising

Most municipalities have them. They are the publishers of magazines that have general interest articles on 'The 3 Ways to Get Spots out of your Carpet' or '5 Things You Should Know About Home Security.' Don't be fooled. These local periodicals are geared toward only one thing: Generating advertising dollars for the publishers.

This motive isn't a bad thing, but the sales representative who comes into your office and tries to sell you on the idea that your payroll services company should advertise in their magazine with a circulation of 20 000 is again selling you something you don't need.

Don't be in it just for the Money

This is a less tangible tip, but it is still worth mentioning. The old adage of not doing something for the money still applies. There's nothing wrong with making a living from your profession, but when you find that you're only in it for the money, it's time for self-examination to determine whether there is something still enjoyable and fulfilling about your profession or if you need to start looking elsewhere for a new opportunity.

Never Apologize for your Fees

Conversely, after talking to you about not being in it for the money, I can't emphasize this enough: never be sorry for how much you charge or propose to charge the client. You spent many years going to school, taking the certification and licensure tests, building a system and an infrastructure intended to keep your business going. Why should you have to apologize or grovel before the client for what you charge to provide exceptional service and results?

If you continually discount your fees or allow yourself to be haggled down to less than reasonable rates repeatedly, you will find that you begin to resent the client and worse you will still not be able support yourself and your firm. A book that examines this problem in detail is *Start with Why* by Simon Sinek.

Another problem with doing this is that you are sending a subtle signal to your client and prospective clients that you don't think your services are really worth that much and therefore, they shouldn't value them for much either.

Don't be Afraid to Fail

Movie director James Cameron once said: 'don't put limitations on yourself. Other people will do that for you. Don't do that to yourself. Don't bet against yourself. And take risk … in whatever you are doing, failure is an option. But fear is not.'

Risking rejection and failure is a good thing. It might lead to discovering some new concept or idea that might work and become an effective resource that can be used in a repeatable fashion.

Hopefully, as you've been reading through much of this book and especially this last chapter, you have found on common theme: Keep trying new things!

THE BARE BONES DO'S TO ATTRACT NEW BUSINESS

What follows are many of the practical and philosophical ideas that I have tried and found effective in business development activities.

Realistically, it takes many years of working in this profession daily to begin to hone and master the concepts I am about to share. I'm still learning myself. I've compiled a list of things that you can do that is considerably longer than the things to avoid doing. This should help create a sense of freedom and experimentation to try something new.

Here is a list of many of the actions to take in business development:

Start before you're Ready

I read that one of the secrets behind British entrepreneur Richard Branson's multi-billion dollar success in nearly every new venture was that he always started before he was ready. Each time Branson began a new business venture, he hadn't yet aligned everything perfectly and instead just wanted to get things going. What would that desire for perfectionism have done had he wanted to make sure he got everything right out of the gate?

Right out of college, I joined a small start-up company in southern Utah that was selling customer-service training programs to various businesses across the county. I was one of three sales reps at the time. We were hired to get new, profitable clients over the phone. The other two sales representatives would spend days working to perfect client call lists and then develop some method for tracking the results. Each day that would pass was another day that the company didn't make any money. Conversely, my natural instinct was to just start dialing for new prospects once I had become familiar with the essentials of what I needed to know from the prospective client call list.

I'm under no illusion that the approach I'd used on the phone was all that effective, but it just had to get the job done. Even that early on, I understood it was about getting results. Many of the details would work themselves out later and sometimes even greater discoveries were being made as things moved along.

Immersing yourself in executing some social media strategy or working feverishly on perfecting the prospective client database might be a sign of a more malignant problem. That problem is fear. Author Steven Pressfield calls it 'Resistance.' This is a very real force in business development. When you think about it, you are putting yourself out there to be rejected, criticized, condescended to and any number of other seemingly negative experiences that will cause you to wilt at the very thought of it all. Why wouldn't the specter of fear come to haunt you from time to time?

One of the fastest cures to fear is action and that means starting before you are ready.

Give Something Away

Professional service firms offer something intangible into the marketplace. The impact of these services can seem ephemeral. Other than the ideas you share, it is important that the prospective client has something they can take away to remind them of the experience. It should be something useful and also laced with reminders of your brand.

Think about the last few times you met with a prospective client. Was it enough that this client went away with some new information from you on how to solve a problem? What about giving the client something to reinforce your brand and company image in their minds?

The item should be something practical. It should also be something that is quality made, especially if it is going to be used by the client regularly. Forget the bobble heads or ugly desk toys. Give them something useful like a pen and pad of paper or one of those neat metal, reusable water bottles. Whatever you send them away with, it needs to be something you know they will reach for when they need it on a regular basis. More importantly, always be sure to have your logo prominently displayed on it.

Give Away Free Information
There is a theme developing here and it involves giving away things for free. Even in our current sharing culture, this can be a familiar refrain: 'If I give away free information, what will the client or prospective client buy from me?'

This works when you understand that you will need to be giving away the *right* kind of information and in the *right* amount. It will be useful information, but it will not be about all of the nuances of what or how you do what you do. It also will not be self-promotional in any way.

This may seem counter-intuitive, but how often do you read advertorials when you see them in magazines? Not as often as the executives in the company paying for that advertisement would prefer. Why is that? It's because it doesn't seem genuine and it usually is still quite self-promoting. The intent is to entice you, but many times it can be frustrating for the target reader. They usually don't do a lot to help the reader, but instead spend most of the space and time working to convince the reader that he or she is deficient in some way and therefore will need to buy the product or pay for a service.

What are some basic ways to give away free information? A way that I have found to work is to write an article for a trade journal in an industry of which you want be associated. The pay can sometimes be non-existent, but the exposure might be tremendous. Just remember, you're not writing articles for your peers, you're writing articles for the people in the industries you want to serve.

An example would be a payroll/human resource specialist who lives in the Pacific Northwest and wants to target many of the lumber manufacturers in the area along with companies that supply resources and services to those manufacturers. He could write a brief article on employee relations, new developments in payment processing technology or other topics. If he wasn't comfortable writing it himself, he could have someone else do it for him internally.

Another example is an attorney who specializes in homeowners' association law is going to put the focus of her writing output on creating articles for the various trade publications that may cross a manager or HOA board member's desk. She is going to keep this article concise and direct, while still building in interesting material for the reader.

A second way that you can give away information to your prospective clients is to write a white paper. White papers have been around for nearly a century and they seem to make sense in business-to-business settings. In some ways, it is similar to an article only it is usually longer than the regular article. Basically, a white paper is an informative piece that takes an authoritative stance dispensing useful information, while at the same time establishing credibility as a specialist in your field. This makes it less and less like an advertorial and more like something the client really could use. These can be available electronically or in hard copy form. Also, keep the writing style conversational in these, as it can be tempting to drift into a professorial tone.

Technology is a Means to the End, Not the End Itself

As I had mentioned, I wrote this book with a focus on something other than technology. Technology and books about how to use it to promote your firm are ubiquitous. Many are useful and full of great information. Frequently, some new technological development is coming to the forefront, enabling more profitable business development. This is a good thing. It might come in the form of a precise data-gathering application, an array of website analytics software or some other application.

Where it becomes detrimental for business development managers and their supervisors is when it becomes the center of attention for longer than is necessary. These are tools for getting the job done and nothing more. Don't fall in love with the tools; fall in love with the process and the results will follow.

Maintain the Long Haul Mindset

I've heard some successful people say that they never want to be the same person they were 7 years ago. In other words, they want to be seen as having progressed and different from the kind of person they were before with new ideas and knowledge. It's not about discarding the old, but rather building upon your base of knowledge and experience continually as you change and grow with your industry.

The quality of results that you provide to the prospective and existing clients will determine whether or not the client returns to purchase from you again in the future. That means you need to keep investing in yourself every chance you get. If that means taking a course to hone your selling skills, do it. If you read reviews on a powerful new book on business relationship development, buy it without hesitation. Listening to audio books and watching new videos on these subjects can be a major bonus for you as well.

Years of doing this on a continual basis will only benefit you as your knowledge and experience continues to stack upon itself all of the advantages for you. This will hone you into a more effective force for building business. The more committed you are to getting smarter for you and your clients, the better off you will find yourself and your clients.

The professional who stops learning new ideas and concepts in business development will foolishly squander his future. It is vital that you never stop learning. If you are in any type of profession that requires any type of licensure or certification, you are already aware of the need for continuing education credits or something similar that requires you attend various state-certified or industry-sponsored events in order to maintain your licensure. However, this should only be the beginning for you.

As I've mentioned before, this book isn't the end all on marketing and selling professional services. Instead, it is intended to be a quick read that allows you to understand and implement its concepts quickly. This book is one more step in the journey to learning new things. Keep it up. You never know where you might obtain the next important concept or idea to help you grow your business. The key is to be humble and maintain an open mind to the knowledge you don't already possess.

Modern-day writer Nassim Nicholas Taleb talks about the concept of the 'anti-library' in his book *The Black Swan*. He examines the idea that the unread books on one's shelf (or in one's digital library) are much more valuable than anything the owner has already read. The reason the unread books are more vital to success than the read ones is that the knowledge you already possess (while important) is what has gotten you to this point in your journey. To go further will likely require learning the knowledge that you do not yet possess to get to the next level of your achievement. If you also consider how calcified many so-called 'experts' become in the level of knowledge they've reached, it becomes clear that having a humble mindset that is always ready to learn will prevent these foolish traps.

So how do you do it?

Well, besides the cultivation of a teachable, humble mindset, I think it is vital to be actively seeking new knowledge. It also means staying away from the realm of certitude. Being certain about anything related to marketing and selling professional services can be a fool's path. The same goes for your professional field. Rather, you should be open to tinkering and experimenting with new ideas and methods of developing your business could lead to another great breakthrough.

Give it a try. You never know what you'll discover.

Your Promotional Materials should look Professional

When I owned my small professional services firm, I was so busy working to develop new relationships and strengthening the ones that I had worked to develop that I never had a lot of time to develop items like color brochures or glossy prints with lots of cool stock photos and copy on them. Instead, I was making and keeping commitments to the prospective clients that led to them becoming existing clients.

My collateral (promotional material about my company), while not the 'sexiest' in the business, was always professional looking, direct and informative. Your collateral should be that way too. Get to the point in your copy and your message, and then really focus on making and keeping commitments.

Attend Various Networking Events and Social Activities

Attend events that will help you grow your business and meet new prospects. If the event isn't essential to building your business, don't kid yourself that you are spending your time effectively and it will somehow indirectly help build your business and client base. However, if you want to participate in these events out of a genuine desire, then do it for that reason.

Also, be wary of the committee trap. Many industry trade organizations and events are mostly volunteer run and therefore, reliant upon unpaid members to participate in planning their events. As should be expected of any volunteer organization, these events and the people who run them are always on the hunt for warm bodies to volunteer and assist with planning, scheduling, recruiting, fundraising and numerous other sundry tasks that make these events more enjoyable. In some cases, serving on a committee to get closer to a prospective client or to draw attention to your firm and the work you are doing may be beneficial. However, it is vital that you are watchful about getting sucked into the proverbial black hole of taking on too many commitments. It always starts out with one minor voluntary obligation you make, then another is added and another. Soon, you will find yourself as chair of the membership committee when all you wanted to do was sign up three of your friends for a golf tournament.

Be vigilant about how much you time you allot for these types of things.

Let Everyone Else see you as an Expert; you are a Specialist

Experts who believe in their own vast body of knowledge run the risk of becoming obsolete. Legislation, regulation, new technologies and trends along with a host of other external forces will be developing outside of your professional practice. Are you ready for those changes? Sometimes these forces will be working in your favor; more often they will be working against you. It's tempting at times like these to kick back and rest on the credibility you've attained and the knowledge you carry with you.

This lax attitude can be found in the tax accountant who doesn't realize he's competing against low cost software until it's too late. This attitude can also manifest itself in the proprietor of a human resource management/payroll company who thinks that companies will always need to outsource and pay for their services. Suddenly, one of their biggest clients had figured out how to send the work overseas or bring it in-house for much less. Now the company owners are scrambling.

Keep your skills sharp. Keep your eyes open.

Focus on Planning, Not your Plan

Dwight D. Eisenhower is credited with saying 'Plans are nothing; planning is everything.'

At first glance that advice might seem confusing. How can you be planning and not have actual plans? You can have a plan and you should have plan. It's the act of planning, the mindset and thought processes connected to actually planning something and most importantly, the agility displayed when one is in the act of planning will always lead you to your desired results faster than setting a detailed, static plan on how to accomplish a complicated task on paper and following it to the 'T.'

For you, it is better to see the process of getting clients as a strategy, rather than a plan. Plans are static; strategies are dynamic. Plans begin to smell and rot almost as soon as the ink is dry on them, while strategies are malleable, fresh and adaptable as it's adherents move through it's ever-changing corridors or shifting competitive battlefield. Plans work better for things that don't change, while strategies work better with people, who do change.

It's in the Details

All of the time, I hear of someone who focuses solely or mainly on 'the big picture.' These people usually can't be bothered by the details and therefore, they try to delegate that work out to others whom they hope will pick up on certain things they would have missed.

Most small-sized to mid-sized professional services providers don't have the luxury of ignoring things like the way the receptionist greets visitors or answers the phone. If it's not a quality greeting, it needs to change immediately. Or how about the perpetual spelling and grammar errors in an assistant's email replies to your clients? Those things matter and they add up over time. Eventually, these things will create a perception from the client or prospective client that there is a certain level of incompetence in your office. You don't need that extra stress.

When you are setting up your practice (or at least examining it after it's been set up), it is vital that you focus in on certain details and then follow them to their logical conclusion, which should be improvement.

Behold the Power of the Hand-written Thank You Note

Every time you pick up your mail, your eyes usually gloss over the envelopes with printed typeface on the front. What happens when it is addressed to you in handwriting? If you're a normal person, you will open it. You want to know who took the time to write you a note. In this world of a million plus fonts, nothing can quite come so close as the intimacy of the human hand and what it can communicate.

Over the years, I've sent over a thousand hand-written thank you notes via snail mail. Personally, I liked writing them in the form of an actual 'thank you' card rather than just on a piece of paper, but either one is effective. When I would visit the offices and occasionally, the desks of some of these recipients, I would discover that these notes were on display. Sometimes they were propped up on a shelf and other times they were pinned to the wall.

Expressions of gratitude should not be suppressed. This applies in personal relationships and professional relationships as well. So often, these clients who received my handwritten thank you notes were treated to a lunch paid for by my company and given an opportunity to talk about them without me talking about myself in return. Doesn't that sound counter-intuitive? Shouldn't they have been the one to send *me* a thank you card? Perhaps, but with how put-upon and unappreciated many of these clients felt, it likely was a refreshing change for them.

Try it out for one month and see what happens.

See the Inner Workings of the Process

This idea applies most to business development managers who have been hired by a professional services company. Giving that business development manager the opportunity to see the process and how certain things are getting done in your office will enhance their understanding.

When I started work at the company where I'd later become an owner, I wasn't originally hired on to be the business development representative. For the first six months, I was brought in to manage the tiny operations department. I think I did a good job, but once the business development manager quit; there was an opportunity to give it a try. It was a great move for me and it seemed to be a profitable move for the firm.

Being able to know the inner-workings of the process we used to create results for our clients was invaluable. It led to more productive conversations between the clients and me. It gave me the credibility I needed to go out into the market and speak with authority to prospective clients about what we could do for them.

If you have a BDM who seems to be struggling with selling certain services your firm has to offer, give him or her a chance to watch how things are being done in that area. It could be that they are too embarrassed to admit they don't know how a certain process should go. There might even be a fundamental lack of understanding about the definition of certain words that you take for granted. Doing this for at least one day every month or two might clear up some potential embarrassment of their own ignorance while still enhancing their knowledge and sharpening their skills.

Focus on Solutions More than the Relationship

I've seen it time and time again. The service provider takes a prospective client on a nice trip (forbidden in some industries and in some states) or offers some other inducement, only to discover the new business was still flowing to me all along. It was hilarious!

Why would I keep getting the business while my competitors were outspending me on lavish lunches, expensive golf outings and so much more? It's quite simple. While they were feeding the client and entertaining them, I was thinking of new ways to solve the clients' problems.

When you are solving the client's problems consistently, the relationship will take care of itself. Yes, I know you're thinking this is so not the sexy solution to getting more clients to sign on with you, but it is the reality. It was my reality and I bet it is your reality too. The days of doing business with someone 'because he's a nice guy' or 'she's a cute girl' are over. So many clients don't really have time to go to lunch with you or take your trip and then solve all of the problems you haven't solved for them. Trust me when I say that the more you focus on solving the clients' problems, the greater effectiveness you will find in your own business solutions.

Focus More on Client Retention

In the award-winning cable television series 'Mad Men,' superstar advertising creative director Don Draper says: 'The day you sign a client is the day you start losing them.' Later, in the same episode, this sentiment is echoed by the lead account executive, Roger Sterling.

This is a lie or at most, a half-truth.

Clients can be a fickle and finicky bunch, but that doesn't mean they get up and fly away at the first sign of trouble. Building your firm and your firm's brand around having the lowest price will always be a recipe for trouble. A client who has gone through the process of sending out requests for proposals or researched various companies that may provide services that could fit their needs or any other deliberate efforts to locate solution providers knows that changing providers at the first sign of trouble is usually a headache. Where the problems almost always begin to appear is when the service provider hasn't taken the proper and necessary steps to ensure the client's needs are being met along the way.

Most clients aren't ready to fire you the first time your firm drops the ball. However, if you continually drop the ball in little ways over the coming months and years by not following through on commitments in a timely manner or returning phone calls within a reasonable timeframe or being careless in how you handle confidential information, you will be fulfilling Don Draper's prophecy.

It has been said that it costs three times more money to lose a client and then go and find another one to replace them than it does to just hold onto the one you already have. It's also been said that your firm will likely need to find three clients to replace the revenue you just barely lost when a client terminated you. This may be true or the facts may be dubious. Regardless, the professional service firms who are in perpetual business growth mode are common. Sometimes they need to master the art of *holding onto* clients before they master the art of getting more clients.

There are things that you should and could do to make it more attractive for your clients to want to stay. Set up basic rules and processes that ensure your firm delivers results in a prompt, professional and repeatable manner. A basic rule like returning a call before the end of the next business day or spell-checking an email before sending it or just checking in on an existing client with a brief phone call may be some of the small things that keep the client aboard longer for the bigger things.

Also, whatever you do, do not wait until the client is ready to fire you before you bring in the big guns. It amazes me how many companies wait until their termination is almost complete before getting the company owner involved in a last minute attempt to salvage the deal. By then, it is always too late and it appears insincere to the client.

You Win Some. You Lose Some. And then you win Some More.

This piece of advice might sound like something an inebriated Yogi Berra would have said. However, it's something I used to say when my company was in a competitive bid situation for a large account and the prospective clients would choose a competitor over our company for whatever reason. Regardless, going into an open bid situation requires that you remember that you will not always win. It is important in these situations to try and remain emotionally detached from the outcome of the proposal you are submitting and the deal you are trying to make. Many times, if you've made a positive impression and you've conveyed your concern and interest in the prospective client's situation, you might be next in line when the prospect goes out to bid again.

Don't stress out when a potential account, whether it is large or small, chooses not to use your services. If you keep doing what you feel you do best, then there should be very little to stop the lost prospective client from calling you within the year if he or she is not satisfied with the current choice.

REVIEW

We have covered much in a short amount of time and pages. My hope is that you felt enlightened and inspired without feeling the least bit overwhelmed. Better business development can happen for you now. You just need to apply the ideas I've shared in these pages. My advice is to plan to review this book and its ideas with the intention of sharing some ideas with another professional.

Business development has been around a long time within professional services firms and as a profession. It takes a special type of person to be an effective business development manager. You are that person if you are doing the job. You have proven you are that special type of person if you've seen the results. However, as I said before, the number one quality each business development manager should possess is the ability and more importantly, the desire to work hard. It takes a genuine interest in other people and it also takes a desire to learn new things almost daily so that you can refine and grow as a representative or the professional who is developing business for your firm.

Never fear rejection. Remember and practice basic communication skills and allow some of those ideas that will assist you in more effective cold calling. It's not about closing the deal as much as it is about getting commitments from the clients. Your involvement in your firm or agency will determine your level of commitment. On top of that, there are the 8 traits for business development success and the tips for getting client commitments that will help you in bettering your business development results.

If you have any questions about this book, please feel free to reach out to me either through my website at www.cameronmclark.com or my email address getcameron@gmail.com. I am also happy to connect for online or over-the-phone conversations. Please use the above methods to reach out to me and I will respond.

Good luck and Godspeed!

I BELIEVE IN YOU

I used to consider myself an optimistic person. Over the years, life and certain failures wore me down and I found that my mind would end up in the pessimists' camp from time-to-time. This usually occurred when things were not going my way in business and my personal life. I had a friend point it out to me one day when we were driving to a nearby town. When he called me pessimistic, I blurted out: I'm not pessimistic, I'm realistic. The poor guy didn't know what else to say to me the rest of the trip.

Since then, while engaging in my work, I have found myself to be a pessimist, an optimist, a realist and an idealist. Sometimes that was all happening in the same project! The point is that it didn't really matter what my outlook on life was, I always was ready to work. Many times, I took action, even when I didn't feel like it. When I did that, the results followed and the positive feelings came. That will happen for you. Yes, you will have your 'down days,' but many of them will be 'up' as well. Regardless, it's about moving forward. Keep moving forward. Don't worry about the upward climb. Just keep moving forward.

I believe in you. Someone needs to tell you that from time to time. You need to know there is someone out there who does believe in you and the work you are doing for your clients. The more you believe in yourself and your abilities, the easier it will be for others to believe in you.

It took me many years to get to this point of believing in myself, even when I owned my own company. When you finish the book, you will look for ways to use some of the concepts outlined. Who knows? You'll likely discover new ideas of your own.

Keep it up!

INVITATION

Did you like the book? I'd love a review on Amazon.

Also, if you'd like more information about upcoming projects, please feel free to visit my website at:

http://www.cameronmclark.com

There you will find books and blog postings about Business Development, Sales and Marketing, Client Retention, Communication and so much more.

RECOMMENDED READING

The following titles might seem surprising in that most of them won't deal directly with business development, sales or marketing. Some of these books do focus more on sales than the others, but there is more to business development than just selling. It's about dealing with people and being effective in persuading them to consider you and your firm as a choice. It's about thinking fast and like a business leader, even when you are not one. Become well rounded. Read more than what is on this list. Brian Tracy has been known to say that leaders are readers. I wholeheartedly believe that.

My hope is that *you* will sample some or all of these books, as they are excellent resources for any business professional who wants to sharpen up his or her people skills or just plain old sales skills.

- 'Hannibal and Me: What History's Greatest Military Strategist Can Teach Us About Success and Failure' by Andreas Kluth

- 'Fooled by Randomness: The Hidden Role of Chance in Life and in the Markets' by Nassim Nicholas Taleb

- 'The Obstacle Is the Way: The Timeless Art of Turning Trials into Triumph' by Ryan Holiday

- 'The Psychology of Selling: Increase Your Sales Faster and Easier Than You Ever Thought Possible' by Brian Tracy

- 'Start with Why: How Great Leaders Inspire Everyone to Take Action' by Simon Sinek

- 'The Power of Nice: How to Conquer the Business World With Kindness' by Linda Kaplan Thaler & Robin Koval

- 'The 7 Habits of Highly Effective People: Powerful Lessons in Personal Change' by Stephen R. Covey

- 'Ditch the Pitch: The Art of Improvised Persuasion' by Steve Yastrow

- 'Ego is the Enemy' by Ryan Holiday

- 'The Black Swan: Second Edition: The Impact of the Highly Improbable Fragility' by Nassim Nicholas Taleb

- 'Selling 101: What Every Successful Sales Professional Needs to Know' by Zig Ziglar

- 'Selling the Invisible: A Field Guide to Modern Marketing' by Harry Beckwith

- 'The Power of Charm: How to Win Anyone over in any Situation' by Brian Tracy & Ron Arden

- 'War of Art' by Steven Pressfield

If you can think of books that are useful, but didn't make it on my list, then reach out to me at getcameron@gmail.com. I'd love to hear from you.

ABOUT THE AUTHOR

Cameron M. Clark is a business development specialist with nearly two decades combined experience in professional services business development and radio broadcasting. Cameron graduated with honors from Southern Utah University with a Bachelor of Science in Communications. In 2011, he cofounded a profitable professional services company, which he sold in 2016 to pursue other interests. Currently, he and his family reside in the American southwest.

www.ingramcontent.com/pod-product-compliance
Lightning Source LLC
Chambersburg PA
CBHW020916180526
45163CB00007B/2752